A Lenten Journey with *Jesus Christ* and St. Thomas Aquinas

I dedicate this book to

The Blessed Virgin Mary,

Patroness of the Order of Preachers

A LENTEN JOURNEY

with Jesus Christ and

ST. THOMAS AQUINAS

Daily Gospel Readings

with

Selections from the Writings

of

St. Thomas Aquinas

REFLECTIONS AND PRAYERS

BY

REV. PAUL JEROME KELLER, O.P.

WITH ADDITIONAL INTRODUCTORY MATERIAL BY

PETER J. MONGEAU

WELLESLEY, MA

www.ChristusPublishing.com

Christus Publishing
Wellesley, Massachusetts
www.ChristusPublishing.com

Father Paul J. Keller, O.P., born and raised in Saginaw, Michigan, entered the Saint Joseph Province of the Order of Preachers after having studied at the University of St. Thomas (St. Paul, Minnesota) and the Franciscan University of Steubenville, Ohio. He completed his baccalaureate in theology and the licentiate in theology at the Dominican House of Studies in Washington, D.C. Ordained to the priesthood in 1993, he spent six years in parochial ministry and teaching at St. Mary's in New Haven, Connecticut. He then studied at the Pontifical Athenaeum of Sant' Anselmo in Rome, for his doctorate in sacramental theology. He has taught at Providence College, in Rhode Island, Franciscan University of Steubenville, and is presently at Mount St. Mary's of the West Seminary at the Athenaeum of Ohio in Cincinnati.

Peter J. Mongeau is the Founder and Publisher of Christus Publishing, LLC.

Publisher's Cataloging-in-Publication Data
Keller, Paul Jerome.
   A Lenten journey with Jesus Christ and St. Thomas Aquinas : daily Gospel readings with selections from the writings of St. Thomas Aquinas : reflections and prayers / by Paul Jerome Keller ; with additional introductory material by Peter J. Mongeau.
   p. ; cm.

   Includes bibliographical references.
   ISBN: 978-1-936855-28-5

   1. Lent--Prayers and devotions. 2. Thomas, Aquinas, Saint, 1225?-1274. 3. Thomas, Aquinas, Saint, 1225?-1274--Prayers and devotions. 4. Catholic Church--Prayers and devotions. 5. Dominicans--Prayers and devotions. 6. Prayer books. I. Mongeau, Peter J. II. Title.

BX2170.L4 K45 2012
242/.34   2012949866

Printed and bound in the United State of America

10 9 8 7 6 5 4 3 2 1

Text design and layout by Peri Swan
This book was typeset in Garamond Premier Pro with Snell Roundhand as a display typeface

Nihil obstat:
Very Rev. Basil Cole, O.P.
Censor Deputatus

Imprimi potest:
Very Rev. Brian Mulcahy, O.P.
Prior Provincial, St. Joseph Province, Order of Preachers
10 June 2012

Imprimatur:
Most Reverence Dennis M. Schnurr, Archbishop of Cincinnati
15 June 2012

CONTENTS

ACKNOWLEDGMENTS

The Gospel passages are taken from the *Lectionary for Mass for Use in the Dioceses of the United States of America,* second typical edition © 2001, 1998, 1997, 1986, 1970. Confraternity of Christian Doctrine, Inc., Washington, D.C. Used with permission. All rights reserved. No portion of this text may be reproduced by any means without permission in writing from the copyright owner.

The citations from St. Thomas Aquinas are from:

Summa Theologiae, Latin and English, translation by Thomas Gilby, O.P. (Blackfriars edition), 60 vols. Copyright © 2006 by Cambridge University Press, 32 Avenue of the Americas #1, New York, New York 10013.

The Summa Theologica of St. Thomas Aquinas, translated by the Fathers of the English Dominican Province (Benziger Brothers edition), 5 vols. Copyright © 1948, 1981 by Ave Maria Press, P.O. Box 428, Notre Dame, Indiana 46556.

Commentary on the Gospel of John, translated by James A. Weisheipl and Fabian Larcher, 3 vols. Copyright © 2010 by The Catholic University of America Press, 240 Leahy Hall, 620 Michigan Avenue NE, Washington, D.C. 20064.

The Catechetical Instructions of St. Thomas Aquinas, translated by Joseph B. Collins. Copyright © 2002 by Scepter Publications, P.O. Box 211, New York, New York 10018.

AN INVITATION FROM SAINT THOMAS AQUINAS

Man is directed to God as his last end. So begins the first answer to the very beginning of one of the world's greatest treatises on Catholic theology, the *Summa Theologiae* of St. Thomas Aquinas. It is an invitation to know more profoundly and to love more intensely the one true God for whom we were created.

As man's last end, God far surpasses man and the grasp of human reason, St. Thomas goes on to explain. Yet, the end must first be known if we are direct our thoughts and actions toward attaining that end (*ST* Ia q. 1, a. 1). If I am to arrive at some foreign city as the destination of my vacation, I must first know about the city as well as the location of the city and what it will take to get there so that I may make plans to arrive there in a reasonable amount of time and all in one piece. Since God is beyond our ability to know him and how to get to him, He has graciously revealed himself and made the way to himself evident. First, he has revealed himself through divine revelation: the Sacred Scriptures and Sacred Tradition. Second, he has shown the way by sending his Son, the Second Person of the Blessed Trinity, the Divine Logos, the Word, to take flesh in our human world: Jesus Christ. Our Lord Jesus has said of himself: "I am the way, and the truth, and the life; no one comes to the Father, but by me" (John 14:6).

God is our Creator and Father. He knows exactly what will give us true happiness. His plan from the beginning of creation was that we should know him and love him as the greatest good that fulfills us as human beings; he has made us to live in communion with himself. The fact of the fall of Adam and Eve, the beginning of human alienation from God, has not been allowed to go unchecked. The Incarnation of Christ as man is proof of that. More so is the passion, death, resurrection, and ascension of our Lord Jesus Christ.

Christ issues an invitation to every human being, even those of us in the byways or who have lost our way in the darkness of this world. It is the invitation to come to the Father through him, through the power of his cross, so as to experience the power of his resurrection. It is an invitation, we might say, to live the human life as fully as possible, a possibility that is unavailable without divine help: grace. Moreover, his invitation possesses a certain urgency. This divine insistence to take up the offer of grace is borne of a love for man who has more than lost his way. It springs, too, from a perfect love that takes upon itself the responsibility to heal and raise up in man what man destroyed of his own free will. Nor is this grace merely something external. It is, rather, the Divine Indwelling of the Trinity in each one's soul, and a share of divine life, making it possible to begin heaven even on earth, as we prepare to the abode of God in the eternity of heaven.

St. Thomas invites us to plumb the depths of God intellectually, but primarily as a means to accept the divine invitation to a communion of intimate friendship with the Blessed Trinity. The short passages taken from just a sample of his vast writings are themselves little "urgings" to seek and find the greatest of all goods so that we might attain to the fullness of human and divine life. As we might expect, speaking and writing about God, about Being itself, the greatest Good and our true end, demands close attention. We will need to ponder more deeply the words of St. Thomas in his conversation with us.

The invitation to contemplate God comes to each one of us daily, in a multiplicity of ways. Yet, Lent is set aside by the Church as a privileged season. It is a time to open ourselves to the deeper workings of divine grace. God awaits our answer to his invitation, our assent, as we pour over these passages from St. Thomas Aquinas.

If St. Thomas as the priest and Dominican preacher and professor wanted all people to know Christ and experience divine grace through the sacraments, how much more does he now beckon us toward heaven as he himself enjoys the beatific vision of God. St. Thomas Aquinas, pray for us, and lead us to the one you so passionately love: the Way, the Truth, the Life.

SAINT THOMAS AQUINAS: A SHORT BIOGRAPHY

The Order of Preachers had been barely in existence ten years when Thomas Aquinas was born in the family castle at Roccasecca, a region of Naples, Italy, sometime in 1224 or 1225. As a youngster, Thomas was educated at the Benedictine abbey of Monte Cassino, having been sent there by his family as an oblate (akin to living as a somewhat temporary monk). In his mid-teens Thomas was sent to Naples to continue his education. It was in Naples, too, that the young Thomas met the Dominicans for the first time.

What breath of the fire of the Holy Spirit must that meeting have begun to kindle in that young pure heart and powerful mind. For barely at the age of twenty, if even that, Thomas asked for the habit of Saint Dominic, much to the objection of his parents. Strange as it may sound to the modern ear, their plan was not only that Thomas was to be a Benedictine monk, but that he would also be the abbot of Monte Cassino. Having Thomas installed as head of the monastery was important to his family for political proprietary reasons. Moreover, we should not fail to consider the dint in the Aquino family reputation if Thomas were part of that newly formed band of friars preachers. Surely, their commitment to itinerancy and mendicant begging for their daily sustenance was too much at odds with the preferred way of life that the monks followed. If Thomas must become a religious, at least he ought belong to an upstanding monastery, especially one that could be useful to his family.

Even so, we find it difficult to fathom Thomas's kidnapping by his mother and brothers to save him from what must have seemed a horribly foolish decision to take the Dominican habit. Bringing him back to the family castle, Thomas was held against his will. His brothers even went so far as to try to dissuade him from his religious vows by imposing a beautiful lady of pleasure in Thomas's room. If Thomas would not renege on his pursuit of holy poverty, perhaps they could force the issue by means of lost innocence and chastity. Surely, the friars would then turn him out. Instead, Thomas turned the woman out of his room, snatching a burning brand from the fireplace. She fled the room screaming. This is the origin of the modern-day Angelic Warfare Confraternity.

A year or so later, the burning love for the Dominicans and their life of study and their brand of preaching still could not be extinguished in the heart of Thomas. By some divine working, the very family that had prevented him from joining the Order of Preachers now conveyed their son to the Dominican priory in Naples in 1245. But the friars in Naples wanted to take no chances on a repeat performance by Thomas's family and sent him to Rome. There, the Master of the Order, as the successor of St. Dominic is called, sent Thomas to Paris where he continued his theological studies. Here he met the great scholar and Dominican, Saint Albert the Great, who was to be his teacher for the next number of years, both in Paris and Cologne. When Thomas returned to Paris in 1252 it was as a priest, to take up a teaching post. It was customary at this time to lecture on the *Sentences* of Peter Lombard, the medieval theologian who had collated in a single, large work a comprehensive view of theology. The *Sentences* was especially important because it brought together the opinions and arguments of the greatest teachers in the Church bearing on nearly every theological concern. Upon completing his own commentary on Peter's *Sentences*, Thomas was made a Master of Theology in 1256.

Thomas returned to Italy in late 1259, where he fulfilled several appointments. First, he went to Orvieto, a city north of Rome and the home of Pope Urban IV, where Thomas composed his famous Mass and Divine Office for the feast of Corpus Christi at the request of the Pope. Here he also completed his writing of the *Summa contra Gentiles*, a work based more on natural reason than on Scripture, useful either for Dominicans going off to mission lands or for the educated laity. In 1265 Thomas was sent to Rome to establish the life of study for the Dominican friars in the very priory where Saint Dominic himself had lived (and where his successors continue to live): Santa Sabina on the Aventine Hill looking across the Tiber to Saint Peter's Basilica and the Vatican. Here he began to compose what is known as his greatest work, the *Summa Theologiae*, the summary of theology. Three years later the sack of Rome saw Thomas return to Paris to take up a teaching post. Then it was back to Naples in 1272, all the time working on his *Summa* and numerous other works. The *Summa* was left incomplete when Thomas died on March 7, 1274, just south of Rome at the Cistercian abbey of Fossanova on his way to the Council of Lyon.

If Thomas is known as one of the greatest scholars and thinkers the Church has ever known, he was more the saint, which is to say that he was a man, a priest, of intense prayer and contemplation. During the last months of his life the ecstasies were more prolonged, particularly while he celebrated Mass. One of the more famous legendary accounts of his many mystical experiences accounts for his complete cessation from all his writing. On one occasion as he was praying early in the morning before a crucifix, as was his custom, he was observed by another Dominican to levitate. Christ addressed Thomas from the crucifix: "You have spoken well of me, Thomas, what should be your reward?" Thomas responded: *"Non nisi te, Domine"* (nothing other than yourself, O Lord). Thomas had been working on the section in the *Summa* on the sacraments, particularly on the sacrament of penance. All his writing came to a halt. Thus, we are left without his complete view on several of the sacraments. Lament as we may this abrupt ending to the greatest of Thomas's works, still we rejoice to ponder the inestimable wealth of all his other writings: homilies, commentaries on philosophy and Sacred Scripture, and theological treatises on every possible subject.

Saint Thomas, the preferred and common doctor of the Church, is the patron saint of students and scholars of all the arts and sciences, of universities and schools, and all who are associated with learning and teaching of all types. Even pencil makers take him as their patron. He is variously referred to as the *doctor angelicus*, "angelic doctor" (due both to his teaching on the nature of angels as well as his perfect chastity), *doctor communis*, "common doctor" (in light of the clarity and commonality of his teaching), and *doctor universalis*, "universal doctor" (because he taught on all subjects).

In his biography of Saint Thomas, Father Jean-Pierre Torrell, O.P., cites a passage from Thomas's own writing that gives us a view into the saint's love of the cross from which Christ spoke to him:

Whoever wishes to lead a perfect life has nothing other to do than scorn what Christ scorned on the Cross and to desire what he desired. There is not in fact a single example of virtue that the Cross does not give to us. You seek an example of charity? *There is no greater love than to give up his life for his friends,* and Christ did it on the Cross. . . . Are you looking for an example of patience? The most perfect patience is found on the Cross. . . . Are you seeking an example of humility? Look at the Crucified One. . . . An example of obedience? Begin following Him who was obedient even until death. . . . An example of scorn for earthly things? Follow behind him who is King of Kings, Lord of Lords, in whom are found all the treasures of wisdom and who, nevertheless, on the Cross, appears naked, the object of mockery, spat on, beaten, crowned with thorns, given gall and vinegar to drink, and put to death (*Explanation of the Apostles' Creed*, article 4, nos. 920–24).

This is the same cross that stands at the center of our Lent and the power of which extends to us in the present moment through the sacraments, most especially the Holy Eucharist. It is the cross, and the power flowing from it, to which Saint Thomas urges us to ponder, indeed, to embrace. May Saint Thomas ever be the inspiration for us to seek only Christ Jesus every day of our lives.

SOURCES: John Inglis, *On Aquinas* (Belmont, Calif.: Wadsworth, 2002); Fergus Kerr, O.P., *Thomas Aquinas: A Very Short Introduction* (New York: Oxford University Press, 2009); Jean-Pierre Torrell, O.P., *Saint Thomas Aquinas: Volume 1, The Person and His Work*, trans. Robert Royal (Washington, D.C.: The Catholic University of America Press, 1996).

THE ORDER OF PREACHERS: A BRIEF HISTORY

The Dominican Order is more properly referred to as the Order of Preachers (*Ordo Praedicatorum*). Constituted by Saint Dominic de Guzman in the early thirteenth century, the Order is composed of friars, nuns, and active sisters as well as lay people. Each of these entities shares in a way unique to itself in the work of preaching the Truth that is Jesus Christ down through the centuries. The fundamental work of the Order has, in one sense, changed little. The friars preach at Mass and other venues such as parish missions. They also teach in university classrooms as well as parish centers. They write, administer parish churches, foreign missions, work for the Vatican and carry out many other works, all for Christ. Their lives are sustained by the Eucharist, the choral divine office, study, devotion to the Blessed Virgin Mary and her rosary, living in simplicity in Dominican priories, silence and contemplation. The cloistered nuns "preach" through their prayer for the work of the Order and the salvation of souls, as well as in the silence of their monasteries and the chanted choral Divine Office. Like the friars, they are devoted to the Eucharist and the Blessed Virgin Mary, contemplation of the Word and the monastic life lived in common.

Following the lead of both the friars and the nuns, the active sisters take the Gospel especially to the schools where they teach, the hospitals and hospices where they care for sick and poor, and countless other missionary works. And the laity give their assistance in every way possible, through prayer and both spiritual and corporal works of mercy.

That the work of the Order has changed little through the ages is due to the vision of Saint Dominic that the world in which our Savior entered is still in need of the saving and life-transforming truth of the Gospel. Truth does not change, and even its conveyance changes little, in spite of the passage of time. Only the accidentals change. Modernity requires that Dominicans, still dressed in their medieval habits of black and white, speak to every person through whatever means available. From parchment to the printed book to the digital; from the pulpit or in the midst of cities; in silent witness or in verbal discourse; the Dominican today continues what Saint Dominic began.

Another reason that the work of the Order has changed little is that the needs of the world are quite the same as those of the thirteenth century—or, for that matter, of all the centuries. The very Incarnation of the Son of God as man is the attestation that we human beings are meant to live, and not just to survive, but to flourish. Created by God, we are re-created by Christ. God has never abrogated his plan for creation and life. Christ Jesus came to give life and to give it abundantly (John 10:10). Christ's life, passion, death, resurrection, and ascension are the re-creative mysteries that make up the Gospel. We experience those mysteries through the sacraments of Christ and His body, the Church. But first comes the preaching, and this is how the Order of Preachers came to be.

The idea for the Order all began when Dominic, already a priest and canon regular in Osma, Spain, accompanied his bishop, Diego, on a northbound diplomatic mission on behalf of King Ferdinand VIII of Castile. They encountered the sect of the Cathars, as they traveled into southern France.

The Cathars are also identified as Albigensians (a name referring to the people of the town and area of Albi, France), and their beliefs as

Albigensianism. Whether we speak of Catharism or Albigensianism, we are referring to the pernicious heresy that has plagued Christianity in various forms throughout her history, be it Manichaeism in earlier centuries or the spiritual Gnosticism of our own day. It entails a set of beliefs that looks more than disfavorably on human nature. The body is despised and only the soul or that which is thought to be spiritual is good. The Cathars, in their anti-Catholicism, prided themselves not only on their rejection of priests and their ministry, the sacraments, and many other Catholic teachings, they went so far as to think of themselves as living the more primitive observance of the Gospel and forced their adherents to a strict following of rules of conduct. In this sense, they appeared to be living more deeply the counsels of Christ: austere poverty, religious zeal, and charity. In reality, they despised all things carnal, even to the point of refusing to reproduce and hastening their own deaths through starvation and suicide. After all, to their way of thinking, souls were like heavenly beings trapped in human bodies and needed to be set free. Even in our own day, this false notion continues to be the basis by which people to speak of their "real" selves as their souls, and their bodies as dispensable, able to be treated in any whatsoever. Abortion and assisted suicide are the modern "anti-sacraments" that are signs of the prevailing propensity to pessimism about the human body.

At one point in their northward journey, Bishop Diego and Dominic stopped for the night at an inn in Toulouse in southern France, where they encountered an Albigensian follower, the owner of the inn where they were to stay. Dominic spent the entire night conversing and debating with him. By morning Dominic had brought the innkeeper to see the truth of the Catholic faith. This event planted the seed in the mind of Dominic that germinated into the inspiration of forming a band of preachers to counter the spread of Catharism already spread far beyond southern France (due in large part to a lack of well-trained clergy and the dearth of Catholic preaching).

Bishop Diego realized that attempts of the prelates sent by the pope to evangelize the Cathars appeared foolish in the face of what appeared to be a greater zeal for gospel simplicity on the part of the very people in error, particularly considering the spectacle of his and other prelates' large retinues. If they were to be taken seriously, the Catholic preachers would need to be just as zealous as the Cathars in their embrace of the evangelical counsels of poverty, chastity, and obedience, but not in the body-hating style of the Cathars. And so the bishop and his priest, Dominic, set off as itinerant missionaries, much like Christ and the Apostles, relying on divine providence for sustenance and perseverance, taking the truth of the Gospel from town to town.

Even with success limited at times, and then the death of Bishop Diego, Dominic continued his preaching, often enough moving his hearers to tears, working miracles, and healing the sick.

Several men, mostly priests, joined him in the work of preaching. Already, he had gathered a group of nuns and established them in a cloistered monastery in Prouille. It was their task to spiritually support the brethren in their itinerant preaching. Little by little, Dominic and his associates came to think about founding an Order dedicated to the work they had undertaken, having vowed themselves to God and following a life in common with a regimen of prayer and theological study. It was Pope Honorius III who finally officially approved this band of learned preachers as an Order in 1216.

What began in Toulouse was soon to spread far and abroad. Within months of the papal confirmation, Dominic had determined to disperse the small community of friars, much as our Lord had sent the disciples out two by two. The brethren objected, fearful that such a move would only destroy this newly begun community. Dominic insisted: "Seed when scattered fructifies, when hoarded, rots," according to early sources. The seed did indeed bear fruit as the Order spread throughout the European continent and beyond. Conservative estimates put the Order at 7,000 friars only forty years after its inception, whereas the number was most likely double that. In England alone, by the end of the thirteenth century there were forty-eight priories and more than 1600 friars.

The government of the Order was unique from the start. Saint

Dominic insisted that the brethren should be directly involved in the organization of their lives in a kind of democratic style. Thus, the friars elect their superiors rather than having them imposed from the top. Whether it is a prior of a local priory, the provincial of a region, or the successor (called the Master of the Order) of Saint Dominic, each is elected by the solemnly professed friars to whose jurisdiction it falls. The Dominicans also have a distinctive usage of the Mass, sometimes infelicitously referred to as a rite. This usage of the Mass was important on account of the missionary travels of the Friars Preachers to countries that maintained particular usages prior to the universalization of the Roman Mass in the sixteenth century by Pope Pius V, also a Dominican. Though not much practiced during the decades after the Second Vatican Council, the Dominican usage is gaining in popularity in our own day, thanks especially to the beneficent facilitation of Pope Benedict XVI.

The emphasis on the life of study is seen in the very organization of the priory (the name given to the place where a Dominican community lives) at the outset. Dominican governmental structure required that a priory have among its members a professor to teach the brethren. Thus, Dominican communities were also schools of theology from which the orthodox teaching of the faith would proceed. Often, priories were established near the university of the city. Friars began to hold teaching posts at the great universities, for example, Bologna, Paris, Oxford, Cambridge, and devoted themselves to writing. Among the early friars, we have Saint Thomas Aquinas who was both a great professor and preacher, and prolific author of philosophical and theological treatises.

The Dominicans were also associated with the medieval Inquisition, as were other religious orders of the time. Perhaps the Order of Preachers stands out in its involvement due to the intellectual character of its members, and particularly to Dominic's zeal in preaching the truth of the faith to the heretical Cathars. Nevertheless, the negative reputation of the Inquisition, a work assigned to the Order by Pope Gregory IX in 1231, made it a less than favorable occupation for the sons of Saint Dominic. That being said, many contemporary histories of the various inquisitions emphasize the positive aspects associated with the work of ensuring doctrinal clarity.

The rosary is associated with the Order of Preachers, as well. Dominican priests, nuns, and sisters wear the fifteen-decade rosary suspended from the belt at their left sides. The fifteen decades correspond to the 150 Psalms that make up the Divine Office from the earliest times of monastic and religious life. There are many artistic depictions of the Blessed Virgin Mary giving the rosary to Saint Dominic, iconic of the preaching of the mysteries of the life of Christ typical of the Order. Each of the decades is associated with some particular mystery of our salvation, and like the Psalms, gives one the opportunity to meditate on the timeless, yet new, works of God present in every moment in our world.

The preaching and teaching work of the Order has continued unabated to our own day, even if at times the numbers of Dominicans has fluctuated. As with any organization, reform is always necessary so as to bring into sharper the purpose of the Order and the means to attain it. The first significant general reform happened under the direction of Blessed Raymond of Capua, Master of the Order during the fourteenth century. Raymond's other claim to fame is to have been chosen by Saint Catherine of Siena as her spiritual director. One can only imagine the direction that Raymond himself received from this valiant woman who was a member of an association of the Dominican lay faithful, but who also was an advisor to popes. Another noteworthy revival of the Order began during the nineteenth century, particularly responding to the political revolutions that caused no little suffering for the Church. Father Jean-Baptiste Henri Lacordaire is credited with promoting this renewal, which was later directed by Father Vincent Jandel, a disciple of Lacordaire and Master of the Order in the mid-nineteenth century.

At the beginning of the nineteenth century, Father Edward Fenwick undertook a Dominican mission in the United States. What began with less than a handful of Dominican priests in the wilderness of Ohio and Kentucky became the Province of Saint Joseph. There are three other provinces in the USA. Fenwick himself was named the first bishop of Cincinnati.

The Order has continued its work of preaching in many forms with the rise of numerous congregations of non-cloistered Dominican Sisters working side-by-side with the friars in missions throughout the world. With many of its members declared saints and blesseds by the Church to assist with their prayers from heaven, every member of the Order seeks what Saint Dominic sought with tears: the mercy of God, both for one's own salvation and for the eternal salvation of every human soul created and loved by God.

THE MEANING
AND CELEBRATION
OF LENT

"During Lent, it is not permitted to decorate the altar with flowers, and the use of musical instruments is allowed only so as to support the singing," the Roman Missal instructs (Magnificat edition, 192). There are no Alleluias during the season, and even the Gloria, that ancient hymn of praise at the beginning of Mass just after the penitential rite, is generally suppressed. The Mass vestments are purple, the Church's sign of penitence. The hymn verses themselves bespeak the need to join ourselves anew to Christ's temptations and sufferings, set to melancholic tones.

The Church has made a drastic turn away from earthly consolations so as to embrace a different kind of joy, described in the first Preface for Lent (the prayer immediately preceding the Eucharistic Prayer).

> For by your gracious gift each year
> your faithful await the sacred paschal feasts
> with the joy of minds made pure,
> so that, more eagerly intent on prayer
> and on the works of charity,

and participating in the mysteries
by which they have been reborn,
they may be led to the fullness of grace
that you bestow on your sons and daughters.

The joy of Lent is the interior peace that comes from the grace of being renewed in Christ Jesus. For those who will enter the waters of baptism at the Easter Vigil, this is the joy of knowing how near one to putting off the sickening "old man" with his sinful earthbound ways of thinking and acting and putting on Jesus Christ (see Ephesians 4:17–24). For the already baptized, the joy of Lent is the opportunity to prepare anew for a deepening of baptismal grace, of a deeper purification and a greater release from the bonds of past sins through prayer, mortification and deeds of charity. It might be something like the joy of the lover who must pass through the interminable period of pre-nuptial engagement so as to arrive at the day of union. In this sense, all of life is like one long Lent, preparing for that glorious day of the grace of our own participation in the Beatific Vision of the Blessed Trinity.

"Each year" we receive the "gracious gift" of Lent. Forgetful human beings, we need this annual reminder, another wake-up call to live life fully. Who knows, but this may be our last opportunity to have a Lent to prepare for the resurrection. If not this year, certainly some year. What a sobering thought! Will I be ready? Have I made the most of my past Lents?

We "await the sacred paschal feasts," the prayer says. That is, we already looking forward to Easter Sunday and being renewed by the sacraments, while at the same time looking forward to the culminating paschal feast, the eternal banquet and feast of the Bridegroom and Bride. In the meantime, we stand vigilant, a kind of lifelong penitential waiting, as guests waiting for the arrival of the Bridegroom to take them into the banqueting hall. When we read the Gospel of Matthew, chapter 25, in this light, we begin to appreciate the necessity for being on our guard and warding off the lulling Sirens of so many material comforts.

Too many people think of Lent as that season of gloom, notwithstanding the rubric disallowing flowers and musical instruments and Alleluias. They focus on what they "must give up" and lose out on what riches they could receive. Hardly unclenching their fists wrapped tightly around earthly delights, they struggle through Lent, dejected by their inability to follow through on resolutions made on Ash Wednesday. We are all prone to this weakness until the grace of a new sanctity sheds its glorious light in the mind showing the value of penance, and the need for deeper prayer, and necessity of loving our neighbors with godly love if we are ever to be truly happy. We do well, in this case, to pray for the grace to love penance more than we love comfort, the grace to hunger for God in prayer more than we long to be understood and accepted by humans, the grace to love without counting the cost more than we desire to be loved.

"With the joy of minds made pure . . . " The human mind, my human mind, a world unto itself, and that which makes me human and makes me recall that we are each made in the image and likeness of God. The mind is made for taking in the true, the good, and the beautiful. So many useless worries; attempts to control the uncontrollable; vain grasps to seize and own privately only appearances of the true, the good, the beautiful; denials of reality, twisting the true, the good, the beautiful into idols that fail to fulfill; these are the abuses of the human mind from which we must be delivered and purified. It is a cleansing process that begins with baptism and culminates in the Sacred Feast of Holy Communion. To let Christ into our minds is to be set free, and thus the need for sacraments, those material realities that effect spiritual changes in my soul.

The forty days of Lent (symbolically in Scripture the number associated with testing and preparation) give way to the fifty days Easter, but the fruits of our Lenten practices must not dissipate, as if our Lent were merely something to be tolerated. Lent is worthwhile to the extent that we are changed, that we become more virtuous. Virtue is a more or less permanent disposition by which we think and act rightly. Passing virtue is no virtue at all. To be "made pure" and "more eagerly intent on prayer and the works of charity" is certainly the intent of the Church for her children during Lent, but with a view to these holy realities taking root in a lasting way, so that "sons and daughters" given her by Christ "may be led to the fullness of grace."

Our temporary asceticism, through grace, transforms us and prepares us for eternal glory. All the flowers of the garden will return in full bloom, Alleluias will resound, the glories of lavish music will reverberate—as we acclaim with the "Angels and Archangels, with Thrones and Dominions, and with all the hosts and Powers of heaven," at the Sacred Banquet: "Holy, Holy, Holy Lord God of Hosts!"

SAINT THOMAS AQUINAS ON PRAYER AND LENT

Often enough when people pray they seek to change the mind and actions of Almighty God. But such a change is patently impossible, for God is, by definition, changeless. He is, in philosophical terms, the Unmoved Mover. In other words, God is the source of change outside Himself while remaining ever all-knowing, all-powerful, all-loving, without beginning and without end. It is our world and ourselves that are contingent and subject to change, while God is the only necessary being. We should not think sadly about the unchangeability of God, for He is utterly happy. It is we, poor creatures, who suffer the exigencies of time and place. We long for the fulfillment of happiness, especially after the fact of the fall from grace of Adam and Eve, and our present condition: living with the effects of original sin.

But what, then, is the purpose of prayer, if not to get what we want from God? Must not God be appeased by our sacrifices, our prayers, our proofs of deserving favors by trying to be good? Isn't there a set formulary of cultic practice by which we can steer God in the direction that think right, and to our liking for this or that? Not in any sense whatsoever!

Prayer (and we include our Lenten prayer and practices in this category) is meant to change us, not to change God, Saint Thomas Aquinas says. Some people equate prayer primarily with asking God for things: for ourselves or for others. While Saint Thomas certainly does not rule out the asking of things of God in prayer, he explains that intercession is not the only reason for prayer. Prayer is, first of all, an act of religion, a part of the virtue of justice by which we pay our debt of honor and reverence to God, who is the source of all we are and have. One aspect of prayer as an act of religion is to obey Christ when He tells us throughout the Gospel to ask of God what we need. "Give us this day our daily bread," Jesus teaches us to pray. Our petition made in trust honors God. We reverence Him when we seek and ask our Father for all that is good, aware that all good things proceed from His hand. Yet, the greater part of prayer is the surrender of our minds and hearts to God, Aquinas insists. In this act, we submit ourselves to God in reverence.

Prayers of petition (presuming that we are asking for true goods) do not change God, but they are effective. While God cannot be used, we enter into His plan of providence when we pray. God uses (in the best sense of that word) us. In other words, God deigns to make our petitions a part of what He had determined. He need not integrate our human participation in the running of the universe; it is an act of His love by which he includes us in the mediation of spiritual and temporal goods. It is much like the father or mother who is honored by a child's insistence on "helping" with chores that only an adult is able to accomplish, and more efficiently without the "help" of the child. Just as the parent dignifies the child by including him or her, so God does with our prayers of petition. Indeed, when we make our petitionary prayers with this attitude, we begin to want only that which God wants, and we are transformed by this dignifying act of prayer. Moreover, our prayers are also reminders to ourselves of our need for divine assistance.

The real benefit of prayer is that we are lifted to God; in our conversing with Him, which often should involve more listening than our own talking, we are deepened in our love of God. Surely, Aquinas would certainly agree with Saint Thérèse of Lisieux's description: "prayer is a surge of the heart; it is a simple look turned toward heaven, it is a cry of recognition and of love, embracing both trial and joy." (See *Catechism of the Catholic Church*, 2558–59.)

Prayer transforms us, for it is impossible to come into contact with God without being changed. The change is proportional to our openness, our disposition, to being transformed by God. In His mercy God hears the prayers even the sinner, Saint Thomas assures in light of the parable of the publican in the temple (Luke 18:9–14), providing that the prayer springs from a good natural desire under grace.

The different forms of prayer that form the basis for much discussion in our own day are almost taken for granted by Saint Thomas. For instance, it is now popular to distinguish between vocal and mental prayer. For Aquinas, the two go hand-in-hand, for one cannot simply speak prayers without engaging the mind, lest prayer become so much empty noise. Such a dichotomy makes no sense for him, for the mind and body are a single entity. Prayer needs both the mind and body. When Thomas distinguishes between supplication, petition, intercession and thanksgiving, he does not imply that these are the only forms of prayer. There is also the prayer of meditation which is a process of reasoning about the truth that leads to contemplation. Contemplation, the highest form of prayer, is a gazing upon the truths of the faith.

It is customary to emphasize the need for more prayer in our lives as we enter the season of Lent. If by this one means that we need to exercise our souls more, for the sake of being more spiritually healthy, Thomas would completely agree. But, just as taking on a regimen of exercise only for a season, only to drop it later and return to one's less-than-healthy state would seem almost ridiculous. Sometimes people do this physically as when they want to lose weight to look good for a special event, and then return to their former ways, only to end up worse off than when they began. The taking up of prayer for Lent is meant to actually be a lasting change in our lives. To see it any other way is to fail to recognize the purpose of Lent and the purpose of human existence. Nothing we do with God is temporary because God is our end. Deeper prayer during Lent is meant to continue. With each passing year, presuming we are graced by God with more time on earth to participate in Lenten practices, is a time for going further than the previous Lent, not to simply take up old practices that we never seem to complete.

Finally, a word about contemplation. Some think that contemplative prayer is reserved for extremely holy people or for monastic types. Nothing could be further from the truth. Contemplation requires a heart of love, and the prerequisite for the heart of love is conversion resulting from the action of divine grace in our lives. Thus, anyone capable of receiving grace and being converted is able to be disposed to the prayer that Saint Thomas describes as the gaze of God Himself. Anyone who as ever beheld another beloved person, who has been caught up in the "stare" upon the object of love, knows something of the prayer of contemplation. There is yet another form of contemplation, a higher form, that is a sheer gift of God for chosen souls, but the contemplation discussed here is of a more simple form. If only we would seek to gaze upon God in this way, especially in the presence of the Blessed Sacrament and after meditating upon the Holy Gospel, we would experience greater transformation in our lives. Heaven is an eternity of this gaze, for it is the Beatific Vision. What better way to spend our time on earth than to prepare for so great a gift! (See *Summa Theologia*, IIa–IIae, q. 83 on prayer.)

ON THE DAILY GOSPEL READINGS

As noted, this book presents daily readings and prayers for every day of Lent, weekdays, and Sundays. The daily readings begin with a Gospel Reading, followed by a selection from St. Thomas Aquinas's writings, a reflection, and a prayer.

The Gospel Readings are from the Roman Catholic *Lectionary for Mass for Use in the Dioceses of the United States of America.* The *Lectionary for Mass* contains the readings for Mass selected from the Bible.

If you were to attend daily Mass during Lent in the United States, you would hear the same Daily Gospel Readings included in this book. For example, the Ash Wednesday Gospel Reading, Matthew 6:1–6, 16–18, is the same Gospel Reading you would hear when you attend Mass to receive your ashes. In fact, on each day at all the Masses of the Latin-rite Roman Catholic Church throughout the world, the same readings are heard in Mass, read in the vernacular language or Latin.

There are two main components of the Lectionary: Sunday and Weekday readings. Sunday readings are arranged on a three-year cycle: Year A, Year B, and Year C. The Gospel Readings for Year A are generally from the Gospel of St. Matthew, Year B are generally from the Gospel of St. Mark, and Year C are generally from the Gospel of St.

Luke. St. John's Gospel is read on Sundays in Year A, B, and C during specific liturgical calendar periods.

The Weekday readings are on a two-year cycle: Year I and Year II. Year I are odd-numbered years and Year II are even-numbered years. The Weekday readings during Lent are the same for Year I and Year II although each day's reading is different. In the book, the Weekday Gospel Readings are also the Weekday Gospel Readings in the Lectionary.

For Sundays in this book, you have three different selections of readings and prayers. Each selection begins with a different Gospel Reading, the Gospel Reading from Year A, B, or C of the Lectionary.

Appendix A, the Calendar for Lent 2013–2022 & Lectionary Cycle, lists the specific dates for the next ten years for Ash Wednesday, the Sundays of Lent, and includes the Sunday Lectionary Cycle for the year. Please refer to the table to determine the current year's Sunday Lectionary Cycle: Year A, B, or C and select the appropriate Sunday reading for the present year.

This book in a small way invites you to pray each day with the Church and your fellow Christians in the world on your Lenten journey with Jesus Christ and St. Thomas Aquinas.

PETER J. MONGEAU

ON THE SELECTED READINGS FROM THE WRITINGS OF SAINT THOMAS AQUINAS

Most of the selections taken from the writings of Saint Thomas Aquinas in this book come primarily from two sources: the *Summa Theologiae* and the *Commentary on the Gospel of John*. The *Summa*, abbreviated here as *ST*, was among the last of Saint Thomas's works and is arguably the most famous. It is divided into three major parts, which requires some explanation. The First Part (in Latin, *Prima pars*, and noted as "Ia") deals with God's existence, his nature, his work of creation of the world, the angels and man. It also considers man's nature. The Second Part generally considers morality, and is itself divided into two parts. Thus, the First Part of the Second Part (in Latin, *Prima secundae*, or Ia–IIae) treats human acts in general, virtue in general, and various forms of law. The Second Part of the Second Part (*Secunda secundae*, or IIa–IIae) considers particular virtues and vices. It is important to understand that for Aquinas, living life to the full and attaining happiness is not a matter of legalistic obedience to divine (or even human) prescriptions, but of embracing the life of virtue which is ordered to happiness. The Third Part (*Tertia pars*, IIIa), which was left incomplete by Saint Thomas, takes in the Incarnation of Christ, the mysteries of his life, death and resurrection, the Blessed Virgin Mary, and the sacraments.

The *Summa* was composed, of course, in a medieval style. Thus, within each major part, one finds numerous general questions (abbreviated as "q") and each of these questions further subdivided into articles (abbreviated as "a"). Thus the first quote from the *Summa* for Ash Wednesday is notated as *ST* IIa–IIae, q. 111, a. 2. This means that in the Second Part of the Second Part of the *Summa*, we look for question 111 ("On Dissimulation and Hypocrisy") and go to the second article, which explains one particular feature of the topic, namely how the two sins are quite the same. Other articles teach about other aspects of these sins.[1]

The *Commentary on the Gospel of John* is also written in a medieval style sometime between 1270 and 1272, again, not long before Aquinas's death. In that work, we find divisions based on each of the

---

1. The majority of the Summa texts are taken from the edition produced by Father Thomas Gilby, O.P. [G] of Blackfriars, Cambridge, with some modifications by this author, and chosen for its readability in order to make the Summa more accessible to the reader. In a handful of cases, certain Summa texts are taken from a somewhat older English edition [Benz.], produced by the friars of the English Dominican Province and published by Benziger Brothers. The choice for a particular translation in each case was made with the reader in mind, with the desire to present what is most helpful while remaining faithful to the ideas of Saint Thomas. Whether from the Summa or some other source, any quoted translated text that has been amended is noted as "modified."

Also noted in citations for the Summa are features that assist in locating the quoted text more accurately and used universally when citing the Summa of Saint Thomas. The "sed contra" refers to an opinion on the subject matter and is given just after the major objections that Saint Thomas raises in each article. The term may be translated as "on the other hand" and give yet another point of view on the issue at stake. Immediately following the "sed contra" is the main body of the article in which Saint Thomas addresses his answer to the problem(s). In the citations it appears as "corpus" for the Latin word meaning "body." Finally, "ad" is the Latin shorthand for the response that Saint Thomas gives to an objection. The modern reader at first may find it jarring to read an article in the Summa because of the format: first, objections are raised, then the "sed contra" is given, followed by the fuller answer to the problem in the "corpus." Only then does the reader find the responses to each of the objections raised at the beginning of the article. With a little practice, however, one quickly becomes adept at reading an article directly from the Summa.

chapters of Saint John's Gospel, with subdivisions called "lectures." For instance, the selection for Thursday after Ash Wednesday is taken from Saint Thomas's commentary, chapter 12, lecture 4. The last number in citations from the *Commentary* refers to the paragraph number in the entire work. Hence, paragraph 1643 in this case.

A complete listing and explanation of each of Aquinas's works is found at the end of Jean-Pierre Torrell's masterful work *Saint Thomas Aquinas: Volume 1, The Person and His Work* (as found in the "Suggestions for Further Reading" at the end of this book.

A S H
W E D N E S D A Y
*and the Days
after Ash Wednesday*

GOSPEL

JESUS SAID TO HIS DISCIPLES:

"Take care not to perform righteous deeds in order that people may see them; otherwise, you will have no recompense from your heavenly Father. When you give alms, do not blow a trumpet before you, as the hypocrites do in the synagogues and in the streets to win the praise of others. Amen, I say to you, they have received their reward. But when you give alms, do not let your left hand know what your right is doing, so that your almsgiving may be secret. And your Father who sees in secret will repay you.

"When you pray, do not be like the hypocrites, who love to stand and pray in the synagogues and on street corners so that others may see them. Amen, I say to you, they have received their reward. But when you pray, go to your inner room, close the door, and pray to your Father in secret. And your Father who sees in secret will repay you.

"When you fast, do not look gloomy like the hypocrites. They neglect their appearance, so that they may appear to others to be fasting. Amen, I say to you, they have received their reward. But when you fast, anoint your head and wash your face, so that you may not appear to be fasting, except to your Father who is hidden. And your Father who sees what is hidden will repay you."

MATTHEW 6: 1-6, 16-18

ST. THOMAS AQUINAS

As Isidore says (Etymologies X), "The word 'hypocrite' is derived from the guise of those who in the theatre come on to the stage with their faces disguised by make-up to suit the look of the person they are portraying, now appearing as a man, now as a woman, in order to take in the audience with their acting." So also Augustine notes (De sermone Domini II, 2), "Just as stage players (hypocritae) *take off other people," i.e., play the part of someone they are not, "the one who plays the part of Agamemnon not really being he, but pretending to be—so in the Church and in all of human life one wishing to appear to be what he is not is a hypocrite. He plays the good man without being one." From this we conclude that hypocrisy is deception. (ST IIa–IIae, q. 111, a. 2 [G])*

REFLECTION

People flock to Catholic churches on Ash Wednesday to receive ashes smeared on their heads and hear the words: "Remember, man, that you are dust, and to dust you will return" (cf. Gen. 3:19). In a world where we idolize the most beautiful bodies and attractive faces, Catholics dare to walk about with the mark of Christ on their foreheads, what to others must appear as a distracting, if not unbecoming, smudge of dirt. Even if one were to wear this cross as an act of religious pride, the "guise" of ashes betrays him, for it is meant to be a mark of humility. Like the man who promptly forgets what he looks like after gazing into the mirror, the one who would feign pride may forget his appearance, but the dirt shows all who see him for what he is as a sinner: dust and ashes.

Ashes, fasting, prayer, and deeds of charity are only hypocritical if we perform them to be seen, like the actor appearing to be someone he is not. Hypocrites deny their sinfulness: "they play the good man without being one." Such is the twisted art of the worst kind of lying: self-deception.

Why are our churches packed on an otherwise ordinary weekday? Grace moves people to desire these sacramental ashes. It is the graced moment of stopping the play-acting and facing the reality of our existence. We, who are created in the divine image, have marred that beauty with our sins. We have disproportionately loved mere earthly things, things themselves made of dirt, more than we have loved the God who created us to enjoy communion with him eternally. And so this wearing of ashes is a mark to help us humble ourselves, to reveal the reality and truth of our fallen nature and our personal sinfulness. It is at the same time a prayer to God to transform us, to restore us to friendship with himself that we who are made of dust and ashes may gaze upon the beauty of his face for all eternity.

PRAYER

Grant, O Lord, that these Lenten observances which you inspire us to undertake may turn us wholeheartedly to you; strengthen our resolve humbly to do all for your glory alone; and may your grace refashion in us the image of your divine Son, who, with you and the Holy Spirit lives and reigns eternally. Amen.

GOSPEL

JESUS SAID TO HIS DISCIPLES:

"The Son of Man must suffer greatly and be rejected by the elders, the chief priests, and the scribes, and be killed and on the third day be raised."

Then he said to all, "If anyone wishes to come after me, he must deny himself and take up his cross daily and follow me. For whoever wishes to save his life will lose it, but whoever loses his life for my sake will save it. What profit is there for one to gain the whole world yet lose or forfeit himself?"

LUKE 9: 22-25

ST. THOMAS AQUINAS

Now every one, as a matter of fact, loves his own life, but some love it absolutely, without qualification, and others love it partially, in a qualified way. To love someone is to will good to that person; so, to love one's own life is to will good to it. Therefore, one who wills what is good without qualification to his own life, loves it unqualifiedly; while one who wills his life some partial good loves it in a qualified way. Now the unqualified goods of life are those which make a life good, namely, the highest good, which is God. Thus, one who wills the divine and spiritual good to his life, loves it unqualifiedly; while one who wills it earthly goods, such as riches, honors and pleasures, and things of that sort, loves it in a qualified way. (Comm. John, ch. 12, 4.1643)

REFLECTION

We have washed yesterday's ashes of repentance from our heads, but the work of Lent has only begun as Christ bids us to take up our cross to follow him. It's still a bit early to have broken the Lenten promises we've made, though if they become merely a matter of some great self-improvement program, perhaps it would be better to fall flat on our face lest we take ourselves too seriously in this matter of reform. After all, either it is God who transforms us, or we are not transformed at all.

"Take up your cross and follow me," Christ tells us. This command of our Lord at once transcends all our self-help programs and immediately strikes at the heart of all our sin: that egoism which refuses to acknowledge God as God, and that man is his creature. He is a beloved creature, exalted on account of being made in the divine image and recreated by grace, but a creature nonetheless—a creature who owes it to God as a matter of justice to worship God as God, or to put it in simpler terms, to let God be God.

As soon as we begin to obey this urging of Christ, we have set along the road of humble surrender and true worship. To take up the cross is to say to him: "I choose to serve you, Lord Jesus Christ. I choose to be yoked to you, my Lord, by means of the cross." It is a choice that ultimately leads away from death and doom and toward life and prosperity (cf. Deut 30:15–20). To assent to the cross is to turn away from our disordered loves, and chiefly our disordered love of self, in order to be made worthy to love God. For the cross that Christ urges upon us is the instrument of transformation, as was his. His cross, and ours as well, is the death to self that leads to divine life and loving communion with God. There is no other alternative, else surely he would have told us.

We have no time for silly self-improvement programs disguised as Lenten observances. We have only time enough to give up our egoism, to follow Christ on the road to life and away from the hellish solitude of pride. Here only will we learn to be fully human, to gain full possession of ourselves. Following him we are at last completely and really alive, flourishing in blessed fulfillment.

PRAYER

Grant me, O Lord, the grace to follow you and take up my cross, loving you unqualifiedly. Increase in me the gift of wisdom that I may see the things of this world for what they are and that I may pursue only that which will bring me to live with you forever. Amen.

GOSPEL

The disciples of John approached Jesus and said, "Why do we and the Pharisees fast much, but your disciples do not fast?" Jesus answered them, "Can the wedding guests mourn as long as the bridegroom is with them? The days will come when the bridegroom is taken away from them, and then they will fast."

MATTHEW 9: 14-15

ST. THOMAS AQUINAS

[Fasting] is undertaken chiefly for three motives. First, to bridle the lusts of the flesh. . . . Fasting is the guardian of chastity, . . . that is to say, lust cools off by abstinence from meat and drink. Secondly, the mind rises more freely to the heights of contemplation: thus it is related of Daniel that he received a revelation from God after fasting for three weeks (Dan 10:3). Thirdly, to make satisfaction for sin; so we read in Joel, "Be converted to me with all your heart, in fasting and weeping and mourning" (Joel 2:12). (ST IIa–IIae, q. 147, a. 1. [G])

[For these purposes] natural reason dictates its need (i.e., fasting) for everyone. Hence fasting in general falls under the command of natural law. However, fixing its time and the manner for the protection and profit of Christian people is a matter for positive laws prescribed by Church authorities. (ST IIa–IIae, q. 147, a. 3 [G])

REFLECTION

Fasting is part of the natural law, St. Thomas tells us, which means that it is not restricted to the practice of Christianity. It is not that eating food is sinful. On the contrary, we are the kind of creatures for whom eating and drinking is meant to be good; it brings us joy. Fasting, and its complement, abstinence, is the voluntary withdrawing from food as a good in order to attain some further end or goal. For

37

example, the athlete might fast from certain foods in order to discipline the body, making it more fit for competition. The pregnant mother fasts from certain foods and beverages in order to protect her baby and ensure his or her development. There are many reasons to fast. But Thomas insists that fasting is for everyone for another aim. It prevents a person from making food and drink more than they should be. In other words, eating and drinking is meant to be a reasonable activity, which is to say that it is governed by reason. In order to attain virtue, one must master the sense appetites, and this includes, among other things, mastery over the desire for food and drink. It is not merely a matter of not eating or drinking, but of eating and drinking according to one's needs.

While the Catholic also needs to fast for these "natural" reasons, the Church mandates fasting and abstinence as an act of vigilant love to help us toward the highest good, to prepare ourselves for union with God. Thus, in addition to bridling the lusts of the flesh, as St. Thomas tells us, fasting takes on a supernatural character. Our fasting serves both as an act of penance (surrendering something legitimately good in restitution for our sins) and as a means of contemplating the Blessed Trinity (emptying our stomachs so as to be free of lethargy and have energy for this most important of human acts).

PRAYER

O Lord, increase in me the desire to undertake holy penances and fasting from food and other goods, so that I may turn from my attachment to earthly things in order to keep my mind and heart fixed on you above all other things and persons. Amen.

GOSPEL

Jesus saw a tax collector named Levi sitting at the customs post. He said to him, "Follow me." And leaving everything behind, he got up and followed him. Then Levi gave a great banquet for him in his house, and a large crowd of tax collectors and others were at table with them. The Pharisees and their scribes complained to his disciples, saying, "Why do you eat and drink with tax collectors and sinners?" Jesus said to them in reply, "Those who are healthy do not need a physician, but the sick do. I have not come to call the righteous to repentance but sinners."

LUKE 5: 27-32

ST. THOMAS AQUINAS

The sacraments of the Church are designed to achieve two effects: to render man perfect in all that pertains to the worship of God as expressed in the religion of Christian living, and also as a remedy to counteract the harmful effects of sin.

[Concerning the latter:] baptism is designed as a remedy against lack of spiritual life; confirmation as a remedy against that weakness to which the soul is subject for some little time after birth; the Eucharist against the soul's proneness to sin; penance against actual sin committed after baptism; extreme unction against those elements of sin which remain, those namely which, whether through negligence or ignorance, are not sufficiently removed by penance; order against the breaking up of ties which bind the multitude into a community; matrimony as a remedy against personal lust and at the same time to make good the losses in the community incurred through death. (ST IIIa, q. 65, a. 1 [G])

REFLECTION

In addition to perfecting us in the worship of God, the sacraments are instruments in the hand of the Divine Physician who has come to minister to the sick. And while so many either witnessed or personally experienced the miraculous healings Jesus worked on the bodies of the sick when he walked the earth, it is not only for physical healing that the Word became man. Christ came then, and continues to come in our own day, to heal us of every sickness of soul, including the ultimate sickness deriving from sin, death. Thus, no one is able to say that he is not sick, that he does not need the physician.

Ironically, the religious leaders in today's Gospel passage could not diagnose their own illness; indeed, they considered themselves to be free even of any symptom of sin. At least the tax collectors and sinners knew their plight, their sickness, and their need for something greater than themselves, for the healing divine love that Christ showed them.

This love of Christ is not to be confused with a passing emotional response. Christ's love, ultimately shown to each one of us in his suffering, death and resurrection, does what mere human love cannot: it heals, which is to say, it transforms the human person from the inside out. Only his grace can reach to the deepest part of the soul, and it is for this that Christ instituted the sacraments for every aspect of every human life, curing our sicknesses, our sins, even the most deadly of them.

Christ Jesus is calling us to follow him anew that he may lead us to union with the Blessed Trinity. He has shown us the way to walk by giving us the sacraments through which we can be assured of growing closer to him. Let us endeavor to make the most of the graces he gives us in the sacramental life.

PRAYER

Lord Jesus, Divine Physician, deliver me from all my sins, especially those hidden ones to which I have become accustomed and therefore blind. Then, enlightened and healed by your grace, grant that I may follow you, and adore you in heaven eternally. Amen.

FIRST WEEK
OF
LENT

GOSPEL

At that time Jesus was led by the Spirit into the desert to be tempted by the devil. He fasted for forty days and forty nights, and afterwards he was hungry. The tempter approached and said to him, "If you are the Son of God, command that these stones become loaves of bread." He said in reply, "It is written: / *One does not live on bread alone, / but on every word that comes forth from the mouth of God.*" /

Then the devil took him to the holy city, and made him stand on the parapet of the temple, and said to him, "If you are the Son of God, throw yourself down. For it is written: / *He will command his angels concerning you / and with their hands they will support you, / lest you dash your foot against a stone.*" / Jesus answered him, "Again it is written, *You shall not put the Lord, your God, to the test.*" Then the devil took him up to a very high mountain, and showed him all the kingdoms of the world in their magnificence, and he said to him, "All these I shall give to you, if you will prostrate yourself and worship me." At this, Jesus said to him, "Get away, Satan! It is written: / *The Lord, your God, shall you worship / and him alone shall you serve.*" / Then the devil left him and, behold, angels came and ministered to him.

MATTHEW 4: 1-11

ST. THOMAS AQUINAS

Christ willed to be tempted; first, in order to strengthen us against temptations. For this reason Gregory [the Great] says in a homily, "It was not improper for our Redeemer to wish to be tempted, who came also to be slain; in order that by his temptations he might conquer our temptations, just as by his death he overcame our death."

Secondly, in order to warn us, so that nobody, however holy, may think himself safe or free from temptation. For this reason also he willed to be tempted after his baptism, because, as Hilary says, "The temptations of the devil are mounted especially against those who have been sanctified, for he desires [that is, the devil], above all, to overcome the holy." For this reason also, it is written, "My son, if you aspire to serve the Lord, be steadfast and sincere of heart, and prepare yourself for temptation" (Sirach 2:1).

Thirdly, in order to give us an example: to teach us, namely how to overcome the temptations of the devil. For this reason Augustine says that Christ "allowed himself to be tempted by the devil, so that, in overcoming these temptations, he might be our Mediator, not only as one who helps us, but also as one who gives us the example."

Fourthly, in order to fill us with confidence in his mercy. For which reason it is written, "We have not a high priest incapable of having compassion on our weaknesses, but one who has been tempted in every way that we are, though he is without sin" (Hebrews 4:15). (ST IIIa, q. 41, a. 1 [G])

REFLECTION

Some mistakenly think of God and the devil as two great but opposite forces: the supreme good versus the absolute evil. But they forget that Satan (or Lucifer) is a limited creature, an angel (though not necessarily the most powerful of angels) who sinned by preferring his own *light* (Lucifer means *bearer of light*) to that of the Trinity. He could not turn his love to his Maker and instead turned it inward, where it has become a never-ending self-loathing. His hatred for God extends to all God's creatures, most especially mankind, made in the image and likeness of God. The humiliation of his self-sought damnation is too much for him and he refuses to suffer it alone. Thus he attacks us.

As if it were not enough that he should suffer and die for us, the Lord Jesus permits this gross indecency by the devil. That the God-made-man, Jesus, should allow Satan in all his hideous pride to tempt him is a mystery concerning which we often pass over too quickly, but whose depths can never be plumbed, as with all the mysteries of Christ's life. On this first Sunday of Lent the Church insists that we ponder the event. St. Thomas gives us four aspects to ponder, all of which center on the fact that we are never alone in facing our temptations, whether the source be the world, the flesh, or the devil. The grace of Christ dwelling in us is the only means upon which we can truly rely in order to be victorious over temptations. In fact, the more that we are driven to call upon the name of Jesus, the more our ancient Foe is defeated and driven back to hell.

If Jesus should be tempted, then with what humility must we bear up under our own temptations. No one is exempt from the battle. Neither is anyone denied the power of Christ to overcome the wicked tempter.

PRAYER

All holy and all-powerful God, grant us the grace of your Son, that we may courageously refuse to be mastered by sin and never give way to any suggestion of evil. Grant us, also, your protection from all the wiles of the Enemy of mankind, that we may live in your peace, and in union with you forever. Amen.

GOSPEL

The Spirit drove Jesus out into the desert, and he remained in the desert for forty days, tempted by Satan. He was among wild beasts, and the angels ministered to him.

After John had been arrested, Jesus came to Galilee proclaiming the gospel of God: "This the time of fulfillment. The kingdom of God is at hand. Repent, and believe in the gospel."

MARK 1: 12-15

ST. THOMAS AQUINAS

The occasions of temptation are twofold. One is on the part of man— for instance, when a man comes close to sinning by not avoiding the occasion of sin. And such occasions of temptation should be avoided, as in the warning to Lot, "Do not stay anywhere near Sodom" (Genesis 19:17).

Another occasion of temptation is on the part of the devil, who always "envies those who strive for better things," as Ambrose says. And such occasions of temptation are not to be avoided. For this reason Chrysostom says, "It was not Christ alone who was led into the wilderness by the Spirit, but all God's children who have the Holy Spirit. For it is not enough for them to sit idle; but the Holy Spirit urges them to undertake something great: which is for them to be in the wilderness from the devil's standpoint, because there can be found there no unrighteousness, in which the devil delights. Again, every good work, compared to the flesh and the world, is the wilderness, because it is not according to the will of the flesh and of the world." Now it is not dangerous to give the devil such an occasion of temptation: since the help of the Holy Spirit, who is the author of the perfect work, is more powerful than the assault of the envious devil. (ST IIIa, q. 41, a. 2, ad 2 [G])

REFLECTION

In the Act of Contrition we pray that we may avoid the near occasion of sin, and so we must. But, as St. Thomas points out, we cannot avoid all temptations since some of them originate with the devil. No one is exempt from these battles. So long as we find these temptations distasteful and do not willfully assent to them, they can do us no harm. In fact, as we resist them in the power of the Holy Spirit, "to undertake something great," they become opportunities for growing in virtue and grace.

Building on the teaching of St. John Chrysostom, St. Thomas wants us to see that the wilderness can be for us a place of great blessing when we rely on the power of the Holy Spirit. Not only was Christ led to the desert, but we are led there as well by the same Spirit dwelling in us who led Christ there. The Holy Spirit is always victorious. This is a great truth on which we can stand secure. When we cooperate with the Holy Spirit, the attacks of the devil are turned upside down; the lush garden of the grace-filled soul becomes for the devil an arid desert for he has no sway here.

Having resolved to embrace the life of prayer, fasting and almsgiving, one may think of Lent as a time of deprivation, as going into the wilderness or desert. But it is the Holy Spirit who inspires holy resolutions, even when they are penitential. This Lenten desert is a necessary component for spiritual development. It is similar to the disciplined training of the athlete. The forces that challenge us, even temptations, are opportunities to grow in the Spirit and experience the victory of Christ over the devil.

PRAYER

Almighty God, you teach us "that neither death, nor life, nor angels, nor principalities, nor things present, nor things to come, nor powers, nor height, nor depth, nor anything else in all creation will be able to separate us from your love in Christ Jesus" (Romans 8:28 RSV). Send your Spirit to help us in our weakness, to make us victorious even in our temptations, so that we may, at the end of our journey, share in the glory of your kingdom. Amen.

GOSPEL

Filled with the Holy Spirit, Jesus returned from the Jordan and was led by the Spirit into the desert for forty days, to be tempted by the devil. He ate nothing during those days, and when they were over he was hungry. The devil said to him, "If you are the Son of God, command this stone to become bread." Jesus answered him, "It is written, *One does not live on bread alone.*" Then he took him up and showed him all the kingdoms of the world in a single instant. The devil said to him, "I shall give to you all this power and glory; for it has been handed over to me, and I may give it to whomever I wish. All this will be yours, if you worship me." Jesus said to him in reply, "It is written: / *You shall worship the Lord, your God, / and him alone shall you serve.*" / Then he led them to Jerusalem, made him stand on the parapet of the temple, and said to him, "If you are the Son of God, throw yourself down from here, for it is written: / *He will command his angels concerning you, to guard you, / and: / With their hands they will support you, / lest you dash your foot against a stone.*" / Jesus said to him in reply, "It also says, *You shall not put the Lord, your God, to the test.*" When the devil had finished every temptation, he departed from him for a time.

LUKE 4: 1-13

ST. THOMAS AQUINAS

Some hold that once a demon has been vanquished he cannot any longer tempt the man concerned to the same or any other kind of sin. Others claim that he can tempt other men but not the same man. This latter view is the more likely one if we take it as referring to a specific period of time; thus, as Luke puts it, "Having finished all these temptings the devil departed from Christ for a certain time." The reasons for this are twofold. One is based on God's mercy, for as Chrysostom says, "The devil does not tempt men for as long as he likes but for as long as God allows; for although he allows him to tempt us briefly, he nevertheless holds him in check because of our weakness." The other reason is based on the cleverness of the devils: thus Ambrose says "the devil is frightened to persist because he fears being often defeated." That, however, the devil on occasion returns to the one whom he has lost is evident from what is said in Matthew, "I will return to the house from whence I came out" (Matt 12:44). (ST Ia, q. 114, a. 5 [G])

REFLECTION

St. Thomas mentions two opposite opinions concerning temptations from a demon that has been defeated. On one hand, Origen thought that once defeated a demon lost his power to tempt the same or any other person. The opposing view was that a demon, even if defeated by some soul, would lose power over that person, but could set about to tempt other souls. Thomas steers a middle course and directs us to think about the experience of Jesus in the desert when he overcame the devil's temptations. It was divine strength by which he defeated the devil, and so it is for us. If we continue to live by divine grace, no future assault of the same temptation can defeat us. Moreover, it is important to remember that God is faithful and does not allow us to be tempted beyond our strength but gives us a way out (1 Cor 10:13). Even if the devil returns to tempt us again in the same area, it is reliance on God alone by which we will continually defeat him, for he is too cowardly, St. Thomas explains, to be repeatedly overthrown.

To make good use of God's grace in the moments of temptation we must deepen in the life of daily prayer and use the frequent opportunities for offering penances, even the seemingly trivial moments of each day. While Lent is a special time for prayer, penance and charity for others, such practices cannot be restricted to this season if we are to vanquish the temptations of the world, the flesh and the devil. Using these weapons we will, without a doubt, grow closer to God. Moreover, it is a good idea to bring temptations into the light by mentioning them in the sacrament of confession. In this way the priest can give particular advice about how to fight against them.

PRAYER

O God, your power infinitely surpasses that of all your creatures put together for all of time; send your angels to help us in the hour of temptation and to put our ancient foe to flight; and increase in us holy fortitude to stand fast against all evil suggestions so that our lives may bear fruit for your greater glory and honor. Through Christ our Lord. Amen.

GOSPEL

JESUS SAID TO HIS DISCIPLES:

"When the Son of Man comes in his glory, and all the angels with him, he will sit upon his glorious throne, and all the nations will be assembled before him. And he will separate them one from another, as a shepherd separates the sheep from the goats. He will place the sheep on his right and the goats on his left. Then the king will say to those on his right, 'Come, you who are blessed by my Father. Inherit the kingdom prepared for you from the foundation of the world. For I was hungry and you gave me food, I was thirsty and you gave me drink, a stranger and you welcomed me, naked and you clothed me, ill and you cared for me, in prison and you visited me.' Then the righteous will answer him and say, 'Lord, when did we see you hungry and feed you, or thirsty and give you drink? When did we see you a stranger and welcome you, or naked and clothe you? When did we see you ill or in prison, and visit you?' And the king will say to them in reply, 'Amen, I say to you, whatever you did for one of these least brothers of mine, you did for me.' Then he will say to those on his left, 'Depart from me, you accursed, into the eternal fire prepared for the Devil and his angels. For I was hungry and you gave me no food, I was thirsty and you gave me no drink, a stranger and you gave me no welcome, naked and you gave me no clothing, ill and in prison, and you did not care for me.' Then they will answer and say, 'Lord, when did we see you hungry or thirsty or a stranger or naked or ill or in prison, and not minister to your needs?' He will answer them, 'Amen, I say to you, what you did not do for one of these least ones, you did not do for me.' And these will go off to eternal punishment, but the righteous to eternal life."

MATTHEW 25: 31-46

ST. THOMAS AQUINAS

Now, against [the] fear of the judgment we ought to have four remedies. The first is good works: "Would you have no fear of him who is in authority? Then do what is good, and you will receive his approval" (Rom. 13:3). The second is confession and repentance for sins committed; and this ought to include sorrow in thinking of them, feeling of shame in confessing them, and all severity in making satisfaction for them. And these will take away the eternal punishment. The third is giving of alms, which makes all things clean: "Make friends for yourselves by means of unrighteous mammon, so that you fail, they may receive you into the eternal everlasting dwellings" (Luke 16:9). The fourth is charity, viz., the love of God and our neighbor, for "love covers a multitude of sins" (1 Pet 4:8). (Catechetical Instructions: The Apostles' Creed, a. 7 [modified])

REFLECTION

There is a soft form of Christianity (if it is Christianity at all) that denies, or at least is willing to "forget" hard teachings such as we hear in this Gospel passage on the last judgment. The fact remains that we cannot alter Christ's word, part of which is that we are responsible for our actions or inactions, whether they are good or evil. Unlike the animals which operate under the weight of instinct, each one of us must give an accounting to God of the life lived because we have been given the gift of freedom to strive for excellence. The saint is one who, aided by divine grace, lives in harmony with God's will and as his intimate and perfect friend.

It is a worthwhile practice to frequently consider the end for which we are made: eternal union with the Blessed Trinity. It is likewise a fearful thing to consider that moment when we will be judged worthy of eternal life or damnation, even if in some circles the mere thought of hell has been damned. Who in his right mind would want to lose such a treasure as God? And so, St. Thomas, the priest and teacher, reminds us of the various means we have at our disposal to heal the wounds caused by our selfish self-pampering and the neglect of the basic human needs of others. First, rather than cower in fear about being judged, St. Thomas urges us to get up and do something: some good deed which is for another and not merely for a good show. Moreover, we should make frequent interior acts of repentance and go to confession, and do penance with a heartfelt urgency. We can be sure that by going to confession any mortal sin deserving eternal punishment is forgiven. Beyond doing good deeds, we should give alms for the poor and the defenseless among us. All of this must be wrapped in the gift of charity, loving another for his own good, and then we shall be sure of our own shame being changed into a robe of glory.

PRAYER

Father of mercy and divine love, your urge your sons and daughters to imitate your goodness to ourselves as we care for those whom you have placed in our lives, near and far; move us, we humbly pray, that we may make more frequent acts of love and humility for the good of others so that we may know the peace of belonging to your household, where you live and reign forever. Amen.

GOSPEL

JESUS SAID TO HIS DISCIPLES:

"In praying, do not babble like the pagans, who think that they will be heard because of their many words. Do not be like them. Your Father knows what you need before you ask him.

"This is how you are to pray:

Our Father who art in heaven,
    hallowed be thy name,
    thy Kingdom come,
thy will be done,
    on earth as it is in heaven.
Give us this day our daily bread;
and forgive us our trespasses,
    as we forgive those who trespass against us;
and lead us not into temptation,
    but deliver us from evil.

"If you forgive men their transgressions, your heavenly Father will forgive you. But if you do not forgive men, neither will your Father forgive your transgressions."

MATTHEW 6: 7-15

ST. THOMAS AQUINAS

We owe God that which we have taken away from his sole right; and this right of God is that we do his will in preference to our own will. Now, we take away from God's right when we prefer our will to God's will, and this is a sin. Sins, therefore, are our trespasses. And it is the counsel of the Holy Spirit that we ask God pardon for our sins, and so we say: "Forgive us our trespasses."

[It] must be known that on our part we are required to forgive our neighbor the offenses which he commits against us. Thus, we say: "As we forgive those who trespass against us." Otherwise God would not forgive us: "Does a man harbor anger against another, and yet seek for healing from the Lord" (Sirach 28:3)? "Forgive and you will be forgiven" (Luke 6:37). Therefore, only in this petition is there a condition when it says: "As we forgive those who trespass against us." If you do not forgive, you shall not be forgiven.

But you may think, "I shall say what goes first in the petition, namely, 'forgive us,' but that 'As we forgive those who trespass against us,' I shall not say." Would you seek to deceive Christ? You certainly do not deceive Him. For Christ who made this prayer remembers it well, and cannot be deceived. If therefore, you say it with the lips, let the heart fulfill it.

But one may ask whether he who does not intend to forgive his neighbor ought to say: "As we forgive those who trespass against us." It seems not, for such is a lie. But actually it must be said that he does not lie, because he prays not in his own person, but in that of the Church which is not deceived, and, therefore the petition itself is in the plural number. It must also be known that forgiveness is twofold. One applies to the perfect, where the one offended seeks out the offender: "Seek after peace" (Ps 34:14). The other is common to all, and to it all are equally bound, that one offended grant pardon to the one who seeks it: "Forgive your neighbor the wrong he has done, and then your sins will be pardoned when you pray" (Sirach 28:2). And from this follows that other beatitude: "Blessed are the merciful." For mercy causes us to have pity on our neighbor. (Catechetical Instructions: The Lord's Prayer [modified])

REFLECTION

God is all-powerful, yet he insists on allowing us the freedom of will to act contrary to his plan. And in so doing, we sin, acting contrary to our happiness. To repent is to allow the grace of God to turn us back toward true happiness and to receive forgiveness for our sins. The extent to which we can experience forgiveness, and therefore true happiness, is somewhat algebraic: forgiveness is granted to the extent we forgive.

Do you have trouble forgiving? St. Thomas anticipates it when he suggests that the one who cannot yet bring himself to forgive someone offense can at least pray in the name of the Church inasmuch as we are members Her. Such a prayer is infallible, for our Lord has taught it to us. In praying in the name of the Church (as *we* forgive), our Father assuredly gives us the grace to personally forgive, the grace of desiring the good for the other. This is no merely human initiative, so we need not worry that it is something that we do on our own. It is God's initiative, the Lord of mercy, who desires that we not only imitate his mercy, but participate in it, even to become mercy. He has commanded it and will never fail to grant the grace of forgiving.

PRAYER

Father in heaven, convert us not only from our sins of commission and omission but also from our small-minded insistence on holding others bound to a punishment that is impossible for us to impose; increase in us the desire to forgive anyone who has wronged us and mercifully loose the bonds that prevent our hearts from your unrestrained love. Amen.

GOSPEL

While still more people gathered in the crowd, Jesus said to them, "This generation is an evil generation; it seeks a sign, but no sign will be given it, except the sign of Jonah. Just as Jonah became a sign to the Ninevites, so will the Son of Man be to this generation. At the judgment the queen of the south will rise with the men of this generation and she will condemn them, because she came from the ends of the earth to hear the wisdom of Solomon, and there is something greater than Solomon here. At the judgment the men of Nineveh will arise with this generation and condemn it, because at the preaching of Jonah they repented, and there is something greater than Jonah here."

LUKE 11: 29-32

ST. THOMAS AQUINAS

As stated in Sirach 10:15, "pride is the beginning of all sin," because thereby man clings to his own judgment, and strays from the Divine commandments. Consequently, that which destroys sin must needs make man give up his own judgment. Now he that persists in his own judgment is called metaphorically rigid and hard: wherefore anyone is said to be broken when he is torn from his own judgment. But, in material things, whence these expressions are transferred to spiritual things, there is a difference between breaking and crushing or contrition . . . in that we speak of breaking when a thing is sundered into large parts, but of crushing or contrition when that which was in itself solid is reduced to minute particles. (ST Suppl. q. 1, a. 1 [Benz.])

REFLECTION

In teaching us how to be contrite, St. Thomas reminds us that the Latin root of the word means to grind or crush. Thus, the heart hardened by sin, the root of which is pride, must be pulverized, as it were. Actually, it is the stony calculus build-up that is crushed so as to reveal the tender heart with which we were created.

The acts of penance of the Ninevites that our Lord refers to in the gospel—the sackcloth and ashes, the fasting, and the supplications to God, undertaken at the preaching of Jonah—were the expression of their interior sorrow for their sins. They allowed the stoniness of their hard hearts to be broken. We have a greater than Jonah in our midst. Our Lord himself calls us to repentance and contrition. Modeling the zeal of the Ninevites, our desire for conversion and for expressing it in acts of penance is to be even greater.

The ascetical practices of Lent are meant to tenderize our hearts. We need penance because our preoccupations with ourselves harden and inure us to the effects our sins have on others and ourselves. How often, for instance, does it happen that someone is mystified that another has taken offense on account of what we consider to be a light matter? Yet, how often do we ourselves grow bitter when dealt some slight? Our penances are to be acts of reparation insofar as these practices turn us away from our selfish and prideful tendencies and toward God. Lent is the graced season of a change of heart, to make God our all.

But even this contrition is not something we do solely of our own accord. It is a great grace. The pulverization of the hardened places of our hearts is a divine work which we ask God to accomplish when we undertake various forms of penance during Lent or in any season of life. He does not destroy our hearts. Rather, he desires that we have truly human hearts, filled with the fruits of the Holy Spirit: charity, joy, peace, patience, kindness, goodness, generosity, gentleness, faithfulness, modesty, self-control, and chastity.

PRAYER

O Lord, you have revealed that you will never spurn a broken, humbled heart (Ps 51). Make us humble and contrite for all our sins, both personal and those of our community and nation. Heal the roots of our sins and grant us the grace of a pure and human heart set on you alone so that, in the company of your saints in heaven, we may one day gaze upon your glorious and loving face for all eternity. Amen.

GOSPEL

JESUS SAID TO HIS DISCIPLES:

"Ask and it will be given to you; seek and you will find; knock and the door will be opened to you. For everyone who asks, receives; and the one who seeks, finds; and to the one who knocks, the door will be opened. Which one of you would hand his son a stone when he asked for a loaf of bread, or a snake when he asked for a fish? If you then, who are wicked, know how to give good gifts to your children, how much more will your heavenly Father give good things to those who ask him.

"Do to others whatever you would have them do to you. This is the law and the prophets."

MATTHEW 7: 7-12

ST. THOMAS AQUINAS

[If] the object of the petition is useful for the eternal happiness of man in that it pertains to his salvation, he merits it not only by praying but also by performing other good works. Therefore, one indubitably receives what he asks for, but when he ought to receive it, "since certain things are not denied us, but are deferred that they may be granted at a suitable time," as Augustine states. The reception of such things may be hindered if one does not persevere in prayer, and so Basil states, "The reason why thou hast sometimes asked and not received is because thou hast asked amiss, either inconsistently, or lightly, or because thou hast asked for what was not good for thee, or because thou hast ceased asking." (ST IIa–IIae, q. 83, a. 15, ad 2 [G])

REFLECTION

Some people think that God hears only some prayers, as if he were deaf at certain times, or uncaring at other times, or too busy to be bothered by the pleas of each one of his children. Nothing is further from the truth. God always listens to our prayers. And just as the loving father gives only what is good to his child, not stone or a viper in lieu of healthy and nourishing food, so our good God can give us only what is best for us. St. Thomas says that one *indubitably*, without a doubt, receives what he or she prays for *when* it is the proper season. There is, of course, no proper season for receiving something that is not for our good, for our true happiness. Thus, we ought to rejoice, or at least be patient, not become dejected or angry, when something appears, on the surface, to go other than our wish or plan. God is in control and he loves us unto death. Moreover he is always protecting us, sometimes even from ourselves and from what is not good for us or others. We must look deeper into the mystery of divine providence to see God's hand in all things. If it appears that some prayer has not yet been granted, such as the conversion of a loved one, or the overcoming of some personal fault or sin, or the healing of a defect, we must continue to trust with persevering faith, and boldly ask yet again. The answer will come, perhaps disguised, and sometimes when we least expect. The proof of this is the crucifixion of Christ and his resurrection. Who could have ever imagined that God would hear and grant our prayer for mercy and forgiveness and eternal life in just this way? "Blessed are you, O Lord, for on the day I called for help, you answered me" (cf. Ps 138:3).

PRAYER

Loving, Provident Father, grant us the unfailing help of your Holy Spirit that we may ever more find in you all that we need, materially and spiritually. Help us with your grace to know that you ever bend your ear to the suppliant prayers of your beloved sons and daughters and draw us ever more into intimate conversation with you, through Jesus Christ, our Lord. Amen.

GOSPEL

JESUS SAID TO HIS DISCIPLES:

"I tell you, unless your righteousness surpasses that of the scribes and Pharisees, you will not enter into the Kingdom of heaven.

"You have heard that it was said to your ancestors, *You shall not kill; and whoever kills will be liable to judgment.* But I say to you, whoever is angry with his brother will be liable to judgment, and whoever says to his brother, *Raqa,* will be answerable to the Sanhedrin, and whoever says, 'You fool,' will be liable to fiery Gehenna. Therefore, if you bring your gift to the altar, and there recall that your brother has anything against you, leave your gift there at the altar, go first and be reconciled with your brother, and then come and offer your gift. Settle with your opponent quickly while on the way to court. Otherwise your opponent will hand you over to the judge, and the judge will hand you over to the guard, and you will be thrown into prison. Amen, I say to you, you will not be released until you have paid the last penny."

MATTHEW 5: 20-26

ST. THOMAS AQUINAS

[In] order to benefit by Christ's passion, one must be likened to him. We are sacramentally conformed to him in baptism, for "we were buried with him by means of baptism into death" (Rom 6:4). Hence no atoning punishment is imposed upon men at baptism, for they are then completely freed by the satisfaction offered by Christ. And since "Christ died once for [our] sins" (1 Peter 3:18), man cannot be conformed to Christ by being baptized a second time. It is therefore right that those who commit sin after baptism should be made to conform to the suffering of Christ by experiencing some penalty or suffering in their own persons. This punish-

ment, which is much less than man's sin deserves, does nevertheless suffice, because Christ's satisfaction works along with it. (*ST* IIIa, q. 49, a. 3, ad 2[G])

REFLECTION

The fact is that we, of ourselves, cannot pay the cost of our sins, not even the least one of them. Nor can we be holier of own accord than the scribes and Pharisees, as our Lord commands in the gospel. Is he then demanding the impossible of us? Certainly not. For he has taken it upon himself to pay off our "prison debt" and give us a share in the riches of his perfection and holiness.

Baptism is the complete cleansing of all sin, both of original sin, in which we are each conceived as a result of the sin of Adam and Eve, as well as of all personal sins. The sacrament of penance is the means by which sins committed after baptism are washed away, and, if they be mortal sins (sins involving grave matter, full knowledge and full consent of the will), the punishment of eternal separation from God is removed. In either case, it is the power of Christ's suffering and death that is brought to bear on us in this moment. Baptism and penance, each in its own way, brings us into contact with Christ and his work of salvation and healing for our souls.

This does not mean, however, that we are free of the need to do penance. Indeed, the Christian must be clothed in the virtue of penance. Such acts are meant to be oblations of love, in much the same way that a spouse who has offended the other seeks to make up whatever he or she can for even the least wrong committed thoughtlessly or selfishly. This, then, is the meaning of being reconciled with my neighbor: that I am quick to recognize my fault and seek to make amends, rather than calculating who is more at fault. It is not that I can simply claim to be contrite for my share. I must enact my contrition, bringing the power of the sacraments to bear on my relationships. The alternative is a frightening prospect: trying to pay off an impossible debt on my own, to the last penny.

PRAYER

O God of justice and mercy, grant that the power of your passion mediated through your sacraments may increase in me the life of grace and virtue, that all my thoughts and deeds be pleasing to you. Let your transforming and indwelling Presence make me more and more into the image of your Son, our Lord Jesus Christ, who suffered and died for sinners, and that I may, as his disciple, undertake penitential acts for the good of neighbor and your glory. Amen.

GOSPEL

JESUS SAID TO HIS DISCIPLES:

"You have heard that it was said, *You shall love your neighbor and hate your enemy.* But I say to you, love your enemies, and pray for those who persecute you, that you may be children of your heavenly Father, for he makes his sun rise on the bad and the good, and causes rain to fall on the just and the unjust. For if you love those who love you, what recompense will you have? Do not the tax collectors do the same? And if you greet your brothers and sisters only, what is unusual about that? Do not the pagans do the same? So be perfect, just as your heavenly Father is perfect."

MATTHEW 5: 43-48

ST. THOMAS AQUINAS

St. Thomas responds to the question, "Is it a necessary part of charity to love one's enemies?" in this way: *Love of one's enemies can be taken in three ways. In one sense, it can mean loving our enemies precisely as enemies, which is perverse and opposed to charity, because it means loving evil in another.*

Or it can be taken as loving them as human beings, but in a general sort of way, and this is what charity of necessity demands: in other words, a man who loves God and his neighbor may not exclude his enemies from this general kind of love.

Finally, we can take it as applied to particular cases; in the sense of a special act of love towards an enemy. Absolutely speaking, charity does not of necessity demand this, for it does not even require it towards every man individually, as being something physically impossible. Nevertheless it is required as an attitude of mind, in the sense that we should be prepared to love even a particular enemy if real necessity arise.

But, apart from the case of necessity, to do this actually and to love one's enemy for God's sake, belongs rather to the perfection of charity. For since charity makes us love our neighbor for God's sake, the more we love God, the more love we show our neighbor in spite of his dislike for us. In the same way, loving someone deeply makes us love his children too, however unfriendly they may be towards us. (ST IIa–IIae, q. 25, a. 8 [G])

REFLECTION

It is an understatement to say that love of one's enemies is one of the most difficult teachings of our Lord Jesus. This is the case precisely because an enemy is perceived to be someone set against what is good. Yet, St. Paul reminds us that it was while *we* were at enmity with God that he reconciled us to himself by Christ's death so that we might be made his friends (Col 1:21). Having been thus transferred from the enemy camp into the kingdom of God, "to be a people peculiarly his own" (Deut 26:18 NAB), we are called to image that same perfection of our Father who has gone to the greatest extreme imaginable for each one of us.

The difficulty in loving an enemy is that he or she acts contrary to us, St. Thomas states elsewhere. But it is precisely this acting as an enemy that ought to grieve us, he says. Nevertheless, even our enemies are human beings, made in the image and likeness of God, and are God's children, capable of eternal happiness. Charity, by its very definition, seeking the good of the other, demands that we want what is good for any child of God. We hate the evil that our enemy perpetrates, but we must want his eternal happiness, just as our perfect Father desires intensely that all his sons and daughters come home to him.

To be sure, such charity is a grace, but far from an impossible grace. It is, in fact, the essence of the Christian life. This is not to say that loving our enemies happens as if by magic. The grace of charity moves us to make a resolution, an act of the intellect, to choose to be Godlike, and begin, even in a small way, with a prayer of blessing for one set against us.

PRAYER

Perfect and loving Father, stir in me the fiery love of the Holy Spirit to live perfectly in you and for you, so that I may imitate the charity Christ has shown me by his suffering and death. Grant that I may love even those who appear to my enemies, for they too are your gifts to aid me in loving perfectly. Amen.

SECOND WEEK OF LENT

GOSPEL

Jesus took Peter, James, and John his brother, and led them up a high mountain by themselves. And he was transfigured before them; his face shone like the sun and his clothes became white as light. And behold, Moses and Elijah appeared to them, conversing with him. Then Peter said to Jesus in reply, "Lord, it is good that we are here. If you wish, I will make three tents here, one for you, one for Moses, and one for Elijah." While he was still speaking, behold, a bright cloud cast a shadow over them, then from the cloud came a voice that said, "This is my beloved Son, with whom I am well pleased; listen to him." When the disciples heard this, they fell prostrate and were very much afraid. But Jesus came and touched them, saying, "Rise, and do not be afraid." And when the disciples raised their eyes, they saw no one else but Jesus alone.

As they were coming down from the mountain, Jesus charged them, "Do not tell the vision to anyone until the Son of Man has been raised from the dead."

MATTHEW 17: 1-9

ST. THOMAS AQUINAS

After having foretold his Passion to his disciples, our Lord had persuaded them to follow the path of his Passion (cf. Matt 16:21). Now in order for someone to go straight along the way, he must have some foreknowledge of the end; just as an archer will not shoot the arrow straight unless he has first seen the target he is aiming at. And for this reason Thomas said, "Lord, we do not know where you are going, so how can we know the way (John 14:5)?" And this is especially necessary when the way is rough and difficult, the journey wearisome, but the end delightful. Now Christ underwent the Passion in order to obtain glory, not for his soul, which he had from the first moment of his conception, but also for his body; according to Luke (24:26), "Was it not necessary that Christ should suffer and so enter into his glory?" to which glory he leads those who follow in the footsteps of his Passion; according to Acts (14:21), "We have to endure many hardships before we enter the kingdom of God." And so it was fitting for him to manifest his glorious splendor (which is to be transfigured), according to which he will configure those who belong to him; as it is written, "He will configure these wretched bodies of ours into copies of his glorious body" (Phil 3:21). For this reason Bede says, "By his loving foresight he prepared them to endure adversity bravely by allowing them to taste for a short time the contemplation of everlasting joy." (ST IIIa, q. 45, a. 1 [G])

REFLECTION

Of the several reasons for the fittingness of the transfiguration, St. Thomas Aquinas here focuses on the antidote for the scandal of the cross both for the apostles and for us. Lest they (and we) think that the road to the cross simply ends there, lest the following of Christ be identified merely with suffering and death, he shows us the ultimate end for which God created each person: a share in the eternal glory of God himself. But Aquinas is careful: the obtaining of that glory first comes through the suffering of hardships, and for us during this season of Lent, the voluntary embrace of prayer, fasting, and almsgiving. There is no easy way to divine glory.

If the apostles needed this counteracting experience in order to endure Christ's crucifixion and their own suffering, surely we do as well. Our own road to sharing in Christ's glory is often fraught with attacks on the faith from without, the terrors of interior, spiritual torments and even the physical suffering we bear in our bodies. For this reason our Lord has given us a share in the Indwelling of the Trinity, the graces of the sacraments, the assurance of divine revelation and the guidance of the Magisterium of the bishops and above all the pope. All of this, strengthened by our time of daily meditation and contemplating the face of Christ in the Scriptures and prayers of the Church, especially in adoration of the Blessed Sacrament, is the necessary means for keeping our focus on the goal of everlasting joy in heaven.

PRAYER

Father, help us to keep our ears attuned to the voice of your Son and our eyes fixed on him in the sacraments, especially the most holy Eucharist, so that we may be strengthened to come nearer, day by day, to the vision of your eternal glory in heaven. Amen.

GOSPEL

Jesus took Peter, James and John and led them up a high mountain apart by themselves. And he was transfigured before them, and his clothes became dazzling white, such as no fuller on earth could bleach them. Then Elijah appeared to them along with Moses, and they were conversing with Jesus. Then Peter said to Jesus in reply, "Rabbi, it is good that we are here! Let us make three tents: one for you, one for Moses, and one for Elijah." He hardly knew what to say, they were so terrified. Then a cloud came, casting a shadow over them; from the cloud came a voice, "This is my beloved Son. Listen to him." Suddenly, looking around, they no longer saw anyone but Jesus alone with them.

As they were coming down from the mountain, he charged them not to relate what they had seen to anyone, except when the Son of Man had risen from the dead. So they kept the matter to themselves, questioning what rising from the dead meant.

MARK 9: 2-10

ST. THOMAS AQUINAS

Men become adopted sons of God by a certain conformity of image to the natural Son of God. Now this is accomplished in two ways. First of all, by the grace of the wayfarer, which is an imperfect conformity; secondly, by glory, which is a perfect conformity: "We are already the children of God, and what we are to be has not yet been revealed; but we do know that when it is revealed we shall be like him, because we shall see him as he is" (1 John 3:2). Since it is by baptism that we acquire grace, while the splendor of our future glory was foreshadowed in the transfiguration, therefore it was fitting that at the time both of his baptism and of his transfiguration the natural sonship of Christ be made known by the testimony of the Father: since he alone together with the Son and the

Holy Spirit is perfectly conscious of that perfect begetting. (*ST* IIIa, q. 45, a. 4 [G])

REFLECTION

St. Thomas explains the importance of the Father's voice at both the baptism and transfiguration of Jesus Christ. Christ is the only begotten Son of the Father, at whose baptism the Father makes known his Son's divinity both by word and the presence of the Holy Spirit in the form of a dove. At our baptism, we are adopted by God as his children on account of our dying and rising with Christ to new life in the baptismal waters. This is no mere name change, for baptism makes us new creatures and gives us a share in the divine nature, insofar as our own limited human nature is able to participate in it.

Our earthly pilgrimage is meant to be a daily drawing nearer to God, being changed from one degree of glory to another (2 Cor 3:18). Christ's transfiguration is a revelation of his divine glory, but it also communicates to us the desire and plan of God for us to share in his glory, which will be made perfect in our resurrected bodies in heaven. Thomas conveys a certain excitement about this when he quotes John's epistle: if now we are children and are interiorly transformed, what shall heaven be like?

The difficulty comes when we realize that we don't live as God's children now. Sometimes the exigencies of this life seem to hold sway, while at other times we give in all too easily to our tendencies toward living more for the self than for God, in God and with God. At such times we may be tempted to discount the reality of our walk in Christ, or the power of his grace at work in us. Such is the devil's work, drowning out the voice of the Father who continually reminds us, in myriad ways, that we are his beloved sons and daughters. Listen to your Father speaking words of love and encouragement as he draws you homeward to share perpetually in his glory.

PRAYER

Loving Father in heaven, let your voice break through the noise of this world's din and the lies of darkness and my own deafness. May your Holy Spirit continually remind me of your great love, shown perfectly in the sending of your Son to sacrifice his life that we all might share in your life and eternal glory. Make your grace burn ever more brilliantly in my soul. Amen.

GOSPEL

Jesus took Peter, John, and James and went up the mountain to pray. While he was praying his face changed in appearance and his clothing became dazzling white. And behold, two men were conversing with him, Moses and Elijah, who appeared in glory and spoke of his exodus that he was going to accomplish in Jerusalem. Peter and his companions had been overcome by sleep, but becoming fully awake, they saw his glory and the two men standing with him. As they were about to part from him, Peter said to Jesus, "Master, it is good that we are here; let us make three tents, one for you, one for Moses, and one for Elijah." But he did not know what he was saying. While he was still speaking, a cloud came and cast a shadow over them, and they became frightened when they entered the cloud. Then from the cloud came a voice that said, "This is my chosen Son; listen to him." After the voice had spoken, Jesus was found alone. They fell silent and did not at that time tell anyone what they had seen.

LUKE 9: 28B-36

ST. THOMAS AQUINAS

As Chrysostom says, "Moses and Elijah are brought forward [as witnesses] for many reasons." The first is this: "Because the crowds said he was Elijah or Jeremiah or one of the prophets, he presented the chief prophets in his company, so that in this way, at least, the difference between the Lord and his servants might be apparent." A second reason is "that Moses gave the Law and Elijah was jealous for the glory of the Lord." Thus, their appearing together with Christ precludes the calumny of the Jews who "accused Christ of transgressing the Law and of blasphemously usurping the glory of God." A third reason was "to show that he had power of life and death, and that he was judge of the living and the dead; by bringing with him Moses who had died, and Elijah who was still living." A fourth reason was that, as Luke (9:31) says, "they were speaking" with him *"of his passing on which he was to accomplish in Jerusalem,"* *that is, of his passion and death. So, "in order to encourage his disciples in view of this," he brings before them those who had exposed themselves to death for God's sake: for, while risking death, Moses had set himself against Pharaoh, and Elijah against Achab the king. A fifth reason is "that he wished his disciples to imitate the meekness of Moses and the zeal of Elijah."* (*ST* IIIa, q. 45, a. 3, ad 3 [G])

REFLECTION

It is often taken for granted that it was because Moses and Elijah were important Old Testament figures that they appeared at Christ's transfiguration. St. Thomas discusses why they, and not some others, were chosen. We should note, for instance, that Abraham and Isaac, great patriarchal figures who appear in the first reading for today's Mass (cf. Gen. 22), are not at the transfiguration. It may seem odd, since, after all, they prefigure Christ's sacrifice as the only Son of the Father. It must have been thoughts such as this that prompted St. Thomas to discuss the matter. Thus we find the reasons he gives (from St. John Chrysostom and St. Bede). The first is one we might easily miss on our own: that the people themselves had thought Jesus was a resurrected prophet, such as Elijah.

The most credible witness at a trial is one who can vouch for someone's identity and authority to act. If Moses, who received the ten commandments from God and gave them to the people, and Elijah, who showed the power of God in the midst of a rebellious people, speak in person on behalf of Jesus as the Christ, the Son of God, then no accusations against the words and works of Jesus from accusers with far less standing have any worth.

Moreover, that Moses returns from the dead, and that Elijah (who had been assumed into heaven in a fiery chariot) appears, is itself a momentous testimony that the saintly dead and the living are subject to Christ. In addition, they testify to the power of the future event of Christ's passion and death as the means of our salvation, about which Jesus himself had told his disciples and continued to teach them.

God always chooses the best way to communicate his truth to us, and this is no less true with the presence of Moses and Elijah at the transfiguration. While we may think of fitting reasons why other Old Testament figures should have appeared with Jesus, clearly these two are unsurpassable, authenticating Jesus' mission and authority—even if the voice of the Father should have been enough.

PRAYER

Lord Jesus Christ, we seek your face and desire to gaze upon you with our own eyes in all your glory. As we must pass through our own time of carrying our cross with you and be purified by your blood and transfigured by your grace, increase in us the virtue of hope that we may one day attain to that heavenly glory which you revealed at your transfiguration. Amen.

GOSPEL

JESUS SAID TO HIS DISCIPLES:

"Be merciful, just as your Father is merciful.

"Stop judging and you will not be judged. Stop condemning and you will not be condemned. Forgive and you will be forgiven. Give and gifts will be given to you; a good measure, packed together, shaken down, and overflowing, will be poured into your lap. For the measure with which you measure will in return be measured out to you."

LUKE 6: 36-38

ST. THOMAS AQUINAS

Man is induced to mercy by the example of divine mercy, following the text "Be ye therefore merciful, as your Father also is merciful" (Luke 6:36). But our Lord commanded this mercy of his disciples, that they frequently forgive the sins committed against them by their brethren, as when Peter inquired, "Lord, how often shall my brother offend against me, and I forgive him? till seven times?" the Lord answered, "I say not to thee, till seven times; but till seventy times seven times" (Matt 18:21–22). Therefore God also very often offers pardon to sinners through penance, especially when he teaches us to pray, "And forgive us our debts, as we also forgive our debtors" (Matt 6:12). (ST IIIa, q. 84, a. 10, sed contra [G])

REFLECTION

When our Lord commands that we are to be merciful as our Father in heaven is merciful, he is not telling us to do this by our own power alone, an impossible task. To be merciful as God is merciful requires something greater in us than we have by nature, for we cannot be like God without a participation in his own nature. This is what divine grace is, the participation in the life of God. Not that we go out to him, but that he makes his home within our souls, the indwelling of the Blessed Trinity, which begins with baptism.

Notice, too, that it is God who initiates forgiveness and mercy toward us. This initiating work is a model for us to follow, but so much more. Since forgiveness and mercy begin with God, we can be sure of our ability to be forgiving and merciful for we do not depend on our own efforts. We depend on his grace for everything. Therefore the work of mercy is not beyond us, insofar as God makes this grace available to us at all times. He does not, for instance, wait for us to be merciful in order to gain his mercy. It is never a question of earning God's love or gifts.

Moreover, God never asks of us more than he himself does. Hence, St. Thomas tells us that the continual availability of divine mercy through the sacrament of penance is the example for us in showing mercy to others. Indeed, we should recognize the hypocrisy of expecting mercy in the confessional all the while refusing to reflect that same mercy in our relationships. It is not that God refuses us mercy when we truly seek it, for he wants us to learn by his generosity. It is we who stifle our own growth as holy men and women when we refuse to learn the lesson of forgiving others.

Finally, it is important to ponder that God's call to perfect holiness by being merciful is the result of his desire that we be happy, for he does nothing contrary to our happiness. Holiness brings happiness, a concept that the world cannot fathom. It is sin that shackles us to unhappiness. In his mercy, God releases us from those shackles. Our mercy toward others releases them so that they might experience the happiness God intends not only for ourselves, but all his sons and daughters.

PRAYER

Lord God, continue your work of transforming our hearts and embolden us who call upon your name and mercy, so that we may be bearers of that same mercy and forgiveness to all whom you place in our lives. We ask this through Christ, our Lord. Amen.

GOSPEL

Jesus spoke to the crowds and to his disciples, saying, "The scribes and the Pharisees have taken their seat on the chair of Moses. Therefore, do and observe all things whatsoever they tell you, but do not follow their example. For they preach but they do not practice. They tie up heavy burdens hard to carry and lay them on people's shoulders, but they will not lift a finger to move them. All their works are performed to be seen. They widen their phylacteries and lengthen their tassels. They love places of honor at banquets, seats of honor in synagogues, greetings in marketplaces, and the salutation 'Rabbi.' As for you, do not be called 'Rabbi.' You have but one teacher, and you are all brothers. Call no one on earth your father; you have but one Father in heaven. Do not be called 'Master'; you have but one master, the Christ. The greatest among you must be your servant. Whoever exalts himself will be humbled; but whoever humbles himself will be exalted."

MATTHEW 23: 1-12

ST. THOMAS AQUINAS

Pride, superbia, *is so named because thereby a man's will aims above,* supra, *what he really is; hence Isidore notes that a man is said to be proud because he wills to appear higher than he is, and he who wills to overstep his bounds is proud. Now right reason requires that a man should reach out to what is proportionate to him. Consequently pride clearly implies something adverse to right reason. This constitutes a character of sinfulness, for, according to Dionysius, to be beside reason is evil for the soul. Consequently, pride is a sin. . . . Pride is a craving for excellence out of [that is, in excess of right] reason. Augustine remarks that it is the perverse desire to be high and mighty. In the same vein he also remarks that it is a bad imitation of God, for it hates being equal with our fellows under him, but wills to dominate them as taking his place.* (ST IIa–IIae, q. 162, a. 1, corpus, ad 2 [G])

REFLECTION

Our Lord says, in the gospel passage, that the scribes and Pharisees have taken their seat on the chair of Moses, meaning that they possessed the power to interpret and teach the Law which came through Moses. They boasted their position, and took on practices and titles that would add weight to their authority. Christ certainly recognizes their legitimate responsibility as teachers, but warns against following their example.

St. Thomas's explanation of pride is clearly evident in the behavior of the scribes and Pharisees. They wanted to appear higher than they were in reality. They did not follow the rule of right reason (clear and proper thinking that accords with objective reality), but allowed their imagination about themselves to gain the upper hand. Sitting on the chair of Moses was not high enough. In their desire to appear holy, to be like God, they overreached their place and thought themselves above the law they imposed. Thus, they could lay heavy burdens on the shoulders of others without lifting a finger to help, all the while decking themselves out as being better than their brothers and sisters.

We must not lose the irony in this scene. Jesus Christ, who is the incarnate Son of God and seated at the right hand of the Father, high above every principality and power, sought only to be clothed in our human flesh. At any moment he could have demanded complete obedience, yet the gospel tells us that he taught with authority, not like the forced teaching of the Pharisees. He embodied the truth he spoke and thus caused his disciples to desire him. He who is truly our "Rabbi" and "Master" never sought titles or social honors. As God's equal, not an imposter badly imitating God, the only chair, the "special place" he sought was to be lifted up on the cross for our salvation.

He comes ever anew to us in the sacraments to teach us the truth about God and ourselves. It is time to put away our prideful ambitions, even the petty attempts to badly imitate God, and embrace the fact of our human existence. God's love for us can transform us into saints, but only if we first embrace our frail humanity and stop chasing the illusory fictions we tell about ourselves.

PRAYER

Lord, may the truth of your love pierce through the false images we have constructed of ourselves and others; make us love only what is true and good so that we may not be trapped in the false world of pride, but embracing your humble cross, lift us up to your heavenly throne. Amen.

GOSPEL

As Jesus was going up to Jerusalem, he took the Twelve disciples aside by themselves, and said to them on the way, "Behold, we are going up to Jerusalem, and the Son of Man will be handed over to the chief priests and the scribes, and they will condemn him to death, and hand him over to the Gentiles to be mocked and scourged and crucified, and he will be raised on the third day."

Then the mother of the sons of Zebedee approached Jesus with her sons and did him homage, wishing to ask him for something. He said to her, "What do you wish?" She answered him, "Command that these two sons of mine sit, one at your right and the other at your left, in your kingdom." Jesus said in reply, "You do not know what you are asking. Can you drink the chalice that I am going to drink?" They said to him, "We can." He replied, "My chalice you will indeed drink, but to sit at my right and at my left, this is not mine to give but is for those for whom it has been prepared by my Father." When the ten heard this, they became indignant at the two brothers. But Jesus summoned them and said, "You know that the rulers of the Gentiles lord it over them, and the great ones make their authority over them felt. But it shall not be so among you. Rather, whoever wishes to be great among you shall be your servant; whoever wishes to be first among you shall be your slave. Just so, the Son of Man did not come to be served but to serve and to give his life as a ransom for many."

MATTHEW 20: 17-28

ST. THOMAS AQUINAS

To strive after ambitious objects is contrary to humility when it issues from confidence in your own abilities, not from confidence in divine help, especially since the more one humbles oneself before God the more one is lifted up before him. Hence Augustine says, "It is one thing to raise oneself to God, and another to raise oneself up against him. He that bows before God is lifted up by him, he that stands up against him is cast down." (ST IIa–IIae q. 161, a. 2, ad 2 [G])

REFLECTION

While St. Mark's Gospel relates that the Zebedees themselves put in their request for special roles in Christ's kingdom (Mark 10:35–44), St. Matthew tells us that it was their mother who intervened. Either way, Jesus asks them whether they can drink his cup of suffering, to which they respond that they can. St. Thomas Aquinas's insight proves valuable for us for we see clearly that, based on Jesus' subsequent teaching, the brothers were acting contrary to humility. They thought they could handle whatever Jesus might ask of them, not because they trusted in God's grace but because they were secure in their own abilities. The first test proved them wrong, for they, as the other apostles did, fled and hid in the Upper Room, save for John (who hid after his vigil at the foot of the cross). Only when they humbled themselves to receive the divine help of the Holy Spirit did they have the courage to do what they had promised, to drink of Christ's chalice.

Notice that St. Thomas does not condemn outright the striving after ambitious things. Such pursuit of great things is only contrary to humility when we rely on ourselves rather than on God's power. Nor did our Lord chide James and John for seeking greatness in his kingdom. Rather, he teaches them in what greatness consists. Nor is it merely a verbal lesson that he gives, for he will lay down his life as a slave for us, to give his very life as our ransom.

To be a saint is a great thing, and surely God is pleased with our desire to be saints, to enjoy eternal happiness and reign with him in heaven. Indeed, there is no other worthwhile purpose for life on earth than to attain to eternal glory with God. Yet, there is only one road, and a rough one at that (cf. Matt 7:14), to our true destination. It consists in doing exactly as Christ did, to become the slave for others in our lives, to lay down our lives for them. To do this, we must take our eyes off ourselves, off our personal and often small-minded goals in life, and look to Christ alone for our entire fulfillment. True greatness, divine greatness, is not measured in grand feats, but in serving well and with love those whom God has placed in our path.

PRAYER

Lord God, we bow humbly before you and ask that you increase in us the desire to serve you with all our hearts and to love and serve each other in you. Make us zealous for doing deeds both great and small with your divine help, but especially grant us the grace of desiring heaven above all other things. Grant this through Christ our Lord. Amen.

GOSPEL

JESUS SAID TO THE PHARISEES:

"There was a rich man who dressed in purple garments and fine linen and dined sumptuously each day. And lying at his door was a poor man named Lazarus, covered with sores, who would gladly have eaten his fill of the scraps that fell from the rich man's table. Dogs even used to come and lick his sores. When the poor man died, he was carried away by angels to the bosom of Abraham. The rich man also died and was buried, and from the netherworld, where he was in torment, he raised his eyes and saw Abraham far off and Lazarus at his side. And he cried out, 'Father Abraham, have pity on me. Send Lazarus to dip the tip of his finger in water and cool my tongue, for I am suffering torment in these flames.' Abraham replied, 'My child, remember that you received what was good during your lifetime while Lazarus likewise received what was bad; but now he is comforted here, whereas you are tormented. Moreover, between us and you a great chasm is established to prevent anyone from crossing who might wish to go from our side to yours or from your side to ours.' He said, 'Then I beg you, father, send him to my father's house, for I have five brothers, so that he may warn them, lest they too come to this place of torment.' But Abraham replied, 'They have Moses and the prophets. Let them listen to them.' He said, 'Oh no, father Abraham, but if someone from the dead goes to them, they will repent.' Then Abraham said, 'If they will not listen to Moses and the prophets, neither will they be persuaded if someone should rise from the dead.'"

LUKE 16: 19-31

ST. THOMAS AQUINAS

[It] is the part of the generous man to be open-handed; another word for liberality is bountifulness, because the bountiful do not hold back but let go. The same point seems to be contained in the term "liberality," since when someone lets something go, he liberates it, from his care and control, as it were, and shows that his spirit is free (liberum) *from attachment to it. (ST IIa–IIae, q. 117, a. 2 [G])*

REFLECTION

Interestingly, the rich man (whose name by tradition is Dives, meaning rich in Latin) calls out from his place of torment in order to seek a kind of liberality for his brothers, although liberality has more to do with money than spiritual goods. Notice, however, that he is still thinking of himself, in a certain sense. He is worried that his brothers, his kinfolk, and an extension of himself, may end up in punishment. If they are warned, perhaps they can avoid the flames of hell. It's not a matter of their conversion, just a matter of their avoiding punishment. Nor is he concerned about the fate of Lazarus. Rather than rejoicing that Lazarus has been relieved of his suffering, part of which Dives caused, he wants Lazarus to do his bidding. No, the rich man has not learned his lesson, even in his place of torment.

Liberality is opposed to avarice, the vice that is centered on "getting and keeping" wealth, as well as loving it too much or taking excessive pleasure in it (*ST* IIa–IIae, q. 118, a. 3). The avaricious individual forgets that the human person is more than the material, that a person has a soul. This vicious way of life becomes a matter of thinking only in terms of the material, of one's body, of comfort and pleasure, of amassing more and more. When one forgets one's own soul, how can there be recognition of another person's soul? Indeed, the word "person" then becomes merely a synonym for another commodity or a liability. Today persons are identified as impersonal and dehumanizing numbers or codes.

The food that the illiberal Dives refused Lazarus was symbolic of all of Dives' piled-up wealth. We all need enough of the goods of the earth to subsist. But we need more. Might we see in Lazarus's longing for food the symbol of our own longing for the bread of life, the Eucharist? Christ, the truly rich one, the Lord of heaven and earth, from whom every good gift comes, feeds us, not with scraps from his table, but generously with his own Body and Blood, Soul and Divinity, so that we might be sated in this life and prepared to share in the bounteous banquet of heaven where we shall behold him face to face. May we, too, be as liberal with our giving ourselves as Christ is with us.

PRAYER

Lord our God, fill our hearts with the grace of liberality towards this world's goods so that we may rightly care for the bodies and souls of our brothers and sisters. Increase our hunger for all that is good and pure, most especially your holy Body and Blood in the Eucharist. Grant that we may enjoy the fruits of heaven where we will enjoy your presence for all eternity. Amen.

GOSPEL

JESUS SAID TO THE CHIEF PRIESTS AND
THE ELDERS OF THE PEOPLE:

"Hear another parable. There was a landowner who planted a vineyard, put a hedge around it, dug a wine press in it, and built a tower.
Then he leased it to tenants and went on a journey. When vintage time
drew near, he sent his servants to the tenants to obtain his produce. But
the tenants seized the servants and one they beat, another they killed,
and a third they stoned. Again he sent other servants, more numerous
than the first ones, but they treated them in the same way. Finally, he
sent his son to them, thinking, 'They will respect my son.' But when the
tenants saw the son, they said to one another, 'This is the heir. Come,
let us kill him and acquire his inheritance.' They seized him, threw him
out of the vineyard, and killed him. What will the owner of the vineyard
do to those tenants when he comes?" They answered him, "He will put
those wretched men to a wretched death and lease his vineyard to other
tenants who will give him the produce at the proper times." Jesus said to
them, "Did you never read in the Scriptures:

The stone that the builders rejected
*   has become the cornerstone;*
by the Lord has this been done,
*   and it is wonderful in our eyes?*

Therefore, I say to you, the Kingdom of God will be taken away from
you and given to a people that will produce its fruit." When the chief
priests and the Pharisees heard his parables, they knew that he was
speaking about them. And although they were attempting to arrest
him, they feared the crowds, for they regarded him as a prophet.

MATTHEW 21: 33-43, 45-46

ST. THOMAS AQUINAS

As Augustine says: "Since God is supremely good, he would not permit any evil at all in his works, unless he were sufficiently almighty and good to bring good even from evil." It is therefore a mark of the limitless goodness of God that he permits evils to exist, and draws from them good. (*ST* Ia, q. 2, a. 3, ad 1 [G])

REFLECTION

In this rather well-known article on the five ways, or so-called proofs for the existence of God, St. Thomas responds to the objection that God does not exist. The objector's argument is one that is commonplace and stumps people of today: if the word "God" refers to something infinitely good, such infinity would seem to "wipe-out" all evil. And yet all can see that evil exists in our world today. Based on St. Augustine's teaching, Thomas explains that God's infinite goodness and omnipotence are such that God can even use evil to some good end. In his *Summa contra Gentiles*, book 3, chapter 71, Thomas gives several examples. It is important to remember the proper definition of evil; it is the absence or privation of some good in a thing or person. For example, a perfectly skilled artist may produce a painting that is defective, not on account of a lack of skill on his part, but on account of some defect in, say, the canvas, or the paint, or the brush. Even our moral evils, though never directly willed by God, may be turned to the good, for others and even for ourselves.

Thus it is that Jesus, the stone rejected by the builders (the scribes and Pharisees), has become the most important stone of the new temple, the Church. It is not that there was a defect in Jesus by which the elders rejected him. The defect was in them; it was their blindness to Christ's divinity that prevented them from surrendering to Jesus. In spite of their blindness, which would lead them to crucify Christ, God's omnipotence and goodness used even this most atrocious of events to bring about our salvation witnessed so marvelously in the resurrection of Jesus from the dead. Our personal resurrection from the dead will happen because Christ rose from the dead, the result of God bringing good out of evil.

There are numerous evils that cross our paths every day. If not the wars in the world, or the murders and poverty in our cities, then various maladies of our bodies and minds as well as rifts in our personal relationships bring this home, not to mention personal sin. In order to avoid cowardly cynicism and turn in on ourselves, we must turn to God and ask for the courage to trust in divine providence and allow God to act in each and every evil situation. The plain fact is that God's love and power and goodness are infinitely greater than all the evils of the universe piled together. Infinitely!

One way to grow in this trust is to gaze upon the crucifix in prayer, an age-old custom of the saints. It is the symbol of divine power in the midst of the worst evil. The refrain of Psalm 105 used in the liturgy of the Word for today urges us to "remember the marvels the Lord has done." Gazing at the crucifix helps us to do this. There we see Love crucified and encounter the divine power of his resurrection. It is possible to bring the power of the cross into every moment of our lives, even into the swirling storms of life or the repeated battles with sin. The cross is powerful because Christ is all-powerful and victorious.

PRAYER

Lord Jesus Christ, I place all my trust in you with the knowledge that you are God and are all-powerful and all-loving. I thank you, even in the midst of my present situation, for you are at work to bring great good out of every circumstance of my life and the lives of my loved ones. Amen.

GOSPEL

Tax collectors and sinners were all drawing near to listen to Jesus, but the Pharisees and scribes began to complain, saying, "This man welcomes sinners and eats with them." So to them Jesus addressed this parable. "A man had two sons, and the younger son said to his father, 'Father, give me the share of your estate that should come to me.' So the father divided the property between them. After a few days, the younger son collected all his belongings and set off to a distant country where he squandered his inheritance on a life of dissipation. When he had freely spent everything, a severe famine struck that country, and he found himself in dire need. So he hired himself out to one of the local citizens who sent him to his farm to tend the swine. And he longed to eat his fill of the pods on which the swine fed, but nobody gave him any. Coming to his senses he thought, 'How many of my father's hired workers have more than enough food to eat, but here am I, dying from hunger. I shall get up and go to my father and I shall say to him, "Father, I have sinned against heaven and against you. I no longer deserve to be called your son; treat me as you would treat one of your hired workers."' So he got up and went back to his father. While he was still a long way off, his father caught sight of him, and was filled with compassion. He ran to his son, embraced him and kissed him. His son said to him, 'Father, I have sinned against heaven and against you; I no longer deserve to be called your son.' But his father ordered his servants, 'Quickly, bring the finest robe and put it on him; put a ring on his finger and sandals on his feet. Take the fattened calf and slaughter it. Then let us celebrate with a feast, because this son of mine was dead, and has come to life again; he was lost, and has been found.' Then the celebration began. Now the older son had been out in the field and, on his way back, as he neared the house, he heard the sound of music and dancing. He called one of the servants and asked what this might mean. The servant said to him, 'Your brother has returned and your father has slaughtered the fattened calf because he has him back safe and sound.' He became angry, and when he refused to enter the house, his father came out and pleaded with him. He said to his father in reply, 'Look, all these years I served you and not once did I disobey your orders; yet you never gave me even a young goat to feast on with my friends. But when your son returns who swallowed up your property with prostitutes, for him you slaughter the fattened calf.' He said to him, 'My son, you are here with me always; everything I have is yours. But now we must celebrate and rejoice, because your brother was dead and has come to life again; he was lost and has been found.'"

LUKE 15: 1-3, 11-32

ST. THOMAS AQUINAS

Through Christ's passion however we are delivered not only from the sin of the entire human race both as regards the sin and the debt of punishment (for Christ paid the price of our ransom), but also from our own sins, provided we share in his passion by faith, love and the sacraments of faith. Thus through Christ's passion we find the door of the heavenly kingdom open. It was this the Apostle had in mind when he wrote, "Christ as high priest of the good things to come, entered once for all by virtue of his own blood, into the Holies, having obtained eternal redemption" (Hebrews 9:11). . . . By his ascension however he led us, as it were, into possession of the heavenly kingdom. (ST IIIa, q. 49, a. 5, corpus, ad 4 [G])

REFLECTION

It bewilders the mind to think that the prodigal son walked out the door of such a loving and generous father. One can almost hear the son slamming the door shut behind him. What is even more astonishing is the open arms of the father as he anticipates his son's return. His open arms are a sign of the open door to the home in which the son once lived freely.

The parable teaches us the effect of sin: shutting ourselves out from our heavenly Father's care, closing ourselves off from union with him. When we make our way back, it is only by the grace of repentance that flows from Christ. He is the only way, the complete truth, and the most real life (John 14:6). It is Christ who has gone ahead and prepared many rooms for us in the Father's house (John 14:3). He has done this precisely through his sacred flesh united to his divine nature, rescuing us even as we have wallowed in our sins. He has bathed us in his blood, and by his suffering and death has carried us to our Father's house. St. Thomas says that Christ's passion is the door to heaven. We might think of those heavenly doors as being fashioned from the wood of his cross.

It is not merely a matter of making some mental claim on Christ by which we once again return to our Father and enjoy union with him. The act of repentance and faith must be enlivened by divine love, a grace that comes from the Holy Spirit. The sacraments were instituted by Christ precisely for this reason, that we might have the divine guarantee of healing and perfecting grace, and that we might become more profoundly rooted in the loving union which the Blessed Trinity holds out to us. To enter the doors of the heavenly kingdom means that we are already beginning to live at home in our Father's house as we await the consummation by which we will fully and eternally dwell there. Until then, let us pray daily from the heart and frequent the sacraments of penance and the Holy Eucharist.

PRAYER

Heavenly Father, everything that we have is your gift to us. Increase in us the knowledge of our true adoption; help us to realize our identity as your sons and daughters. May your Holy Spirit more thoroughly permeate our souls and lead us to the joy of your heavenly kingdom where we shall enjoy the beauty of your house for eternity. Amen.

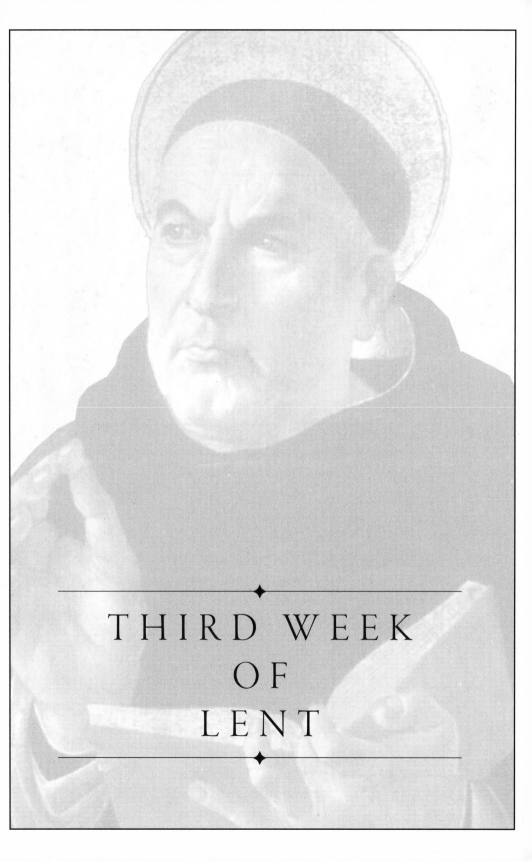

THIRD WEEK
OF
LENT

GOSPEL

Jesus came to a town of Samaria called Sychar, near the plot of land that Jacob had given to his son Joseph. Jacob's well was there. Jesus, tired from his journey, sat down there at the well. It was about noon.

A woman of Samaria came to draw water. Jesus said to her, "Give me a drink." His disciples had gone into the town to buy food. The Samaritan woman said to him, "How can you, a Jew, ask me, a Samaritan woman, for a drink?" — For Jews use nothing in common with Samaritans. — Jesus answered and said to her, "If you knew the gift of God and who is saying to you, 'Give me a drink,' you would have asked him and he would have given you living water." The woman said to him, "Sir, you do not even have a bucket and the cistern is deep; where then can you get this living water? Are you greater than our father Jacob, who gave us this cistern and drank from it himself with his children and his flocks?" Jesus answered and said to her, "Everyone who drinks this water will be thirsty again; but whoever drinks the water I shall give will never thirst; the water I shall give will become in him a spring of water welling up to eternal life." The woman said to him, "Sir, give me this water, so that I may not be thirsty or have to keep coming here to draw water."

Jesus said to her, "Go call your husband and come back." The woman answered and said to him, "I do not have a husband." Jesus answered her, "You are right in saying, 'I do not have a husband.' For you have had five husbands, and the one you have now is not your husband. What you have said is true." The woman said to him, "Sir, I can see that you are a prophet. Our ancestors worshiped on this mountain; but you people say that the place to worship is in Jerusalem." Jesus said to her, "Believe me, woman, the hour is coming when you will worship the Father neither on this mountain nor in Jerusalem. You people worship what you do not understand; we worship what we understand, because salvation is from the Jews. But the hour is coming, and is now here, when true worshipers will worship the Father in Spirit and truth; and indeed the Father seeks such people to worship him. God is Spirit, and those who worship him must worship in Spirit and truth." The woman said to him, "I know that the Messiah is coming, the one called the Christ; when he comes, he will tell us everything." Jesus said to her, "I am he, the one speaking with you."

At that moment his disciples returned, and were amazed that he was talking with a woman, but still no one said, "What are you looking for?" or "Why are you talking with her?" The woman left her water jar and went into the town and said to the people, "Come see a man who told me everything I have done. Could he possibly be the Christ?" They went out of the town and came to him. Meanwhile, the disciples urged him, "Rabbi, eat." But he said to them, "I have food to eat of which you do not know." So the disciples said to one another, "Could someone have brought him something to eat?" Jesus said to them, "My food is to do the will of the one who sent me and to finish his work. Do you not say, 'In four months the harvest will be here'? I tell you, look up and see the fields ripe for the harvest. The reaper is already receiving payment and gathering crops for eternal life, so that the sower and reaper can rejoice together. For here the saying is verified that 'One sows and another reaps.' I sent you to reap what you have not worked for; others have done the work, and you are sharing the fruits of their work."

Many of the Samaritans of that town began to believe in him because of the word of the woman who testified, "He told me everything I have done." When the Samaritans came to him, they invited him to stay with them; and he stayed there two days. Many more began to believe in him because of his word, and they said to the woman, "We no longer believe because of your word; for we have heard for ourselves, and we know that this is truly the savior of the world."

JOHN 4: 5-42

Shorter form: JOHN 4:5-15, 19b-26, 39a, 40-42
Longer form may be optionally read on any day in the third week of Lent

ST. THOMAS AQUINAS

Now water is of two kinds: living and non-living. Non-living water is water which is not connected or united with the source from which it springs, but is collected from the rain or in other ways into ponds and cisterns, and there it stands, separated from its source. But living water is connected with its source and flows from it. So according to this understanding, the grace of the Holy Spirit is correctly called living water, because the grace of the Holy Spirit is given to man in such a way that the source itself of the grace is also given, that is, the Holy Spirit. Indeed, grace is given by the Holy Spirit: "The love of God is poured out into our hearts by the Holy Spirit, who has been given to us" (Rom 5:5). For the Holy Spirit is the unfailing fountain from whom all gifts of grace flow: "One and the same Spirit does all these things" (1 Cor 12:11). And so, if anyone has a gift of the Holy Spirit without having the Spirit, the water is not united with its source, and so is not living but dead: "Faith without works is dead" (James 2:20). (Comm. John, ch. 4, 2.577)

REFLECTION

There are two ways to live. One way is to rely only on human nature alone, as if God does not exist, as if all that matters are the things of this world. One runs after youth, or health, or beauty, or wealth of one sort or another. It is like having only the water to drink that is collected in reservoirs and man-made tanks. Sooner or later it will run out, or stagnate.

The other way to live, to really live (for, truth be told, the former is not living at all) is to become alive interiorly with the drive that comes from the indwelling of the Holy Spirit. One runs after eternal life, and lives by charity, divine grace, and the gifts of the Holy Spirit. It is like having an unending source of water that is ever ready to quench our deepest thirsts. Such is the water that Christ has come to give us. He first immerses us in this water of life in the sacrament of baptism and renews it in the sacraments by which we are made to flourish.

Life on earth is good, and its water is good, but it's not enough.

God did not make us to simply live on this planet and do a few things or have a few pleasures and then die. He made us for true and lasting happiness, which, on account of their very being, the things of this world can never provide. The norm of true human living is not to be judged by the way of life of the majority. True and full human living consists in partaking of the revelation Christ has given, namely, to know, love and serve God, to live in him and to have his Spirit living in us. This is the living water—not of this world—that Christ wanted to give to the Samaritan woman and that he wants to give to us.

PRAYER

Lord Jesus Christ, give me to drink of the life giving water of the Holy Spirit. May I thirst ever more and more each day for the Holy Spirit's life and dynamism and not take for granted my Christian life. Deepen in me the works and gifts of the Spirit that I may be truly alive from within. Amen.

GOSPEL

Since the Passover of the Jews was near, Jesus went up to Jerusalem. He found in the temple area those who sold oxen, sheep and doves, as well as the money changers seated there. He made a whip out of cords and drove them all out of the temple area, with sheep and oxen, and spilled the coins of the money changers and overturned their tables, and to those who sold doves he said, "Take these out of here, and stop making my Father's house a marketplace." His disciples recalled the words of Scripture, *Zeal for your house will consume me.* At this the Jews answered and said to him, "What sign can you show us for doing this?" Jesus answered and said to them, "Destroy this temple and in three days I will raise it up." The Jews said, "This temple has been under construction for forty-six years, and you will raise it up in three days?" But he was speaking about the temple of his body. Therefore, when he was raised from the dead, his disciples remembered that he had said this, and they came to believe the Scripture and the word Jesus had spoken.

While he was in Jerusalem for the feast of Passover, many began to believe in his name when they saw the signs he was doing. But Jesus would not trust himself to them because he knew them all, and did not need anyone to testify about human nature. He himself understood it well.

JOHN 2: 13-25

ST. THOMAS AQUINAS

Then when [John] says, "His disciples then remembered," he sets down a prophecy which was written in Psalm 69: "Zeal for your house consumes me." Here we should remark that zeal, properly speaking, signifies an intensity of love, whereby the one who loves intensely does not tolerate anything which is repugnant to his love. . . . Thus, properly speaking, one is said to have zeal for God who cannot patiently endure anything contrary to the honor of God, whom he loves above all else: "I have been very zealous for the Lord God of hosts" (1 Kings 19:10). Now we should love the house of the Lord, according to the Psalm (26:8): "O Lord, I have loved the beauty of your house." Indeed, we should love it so much that our zeal consumes us, so that if we notice anything amiss being done, we should try to eliminate it, no matter how dear to us are those who are doing it; nor should we fear any evils that we might have to endure as a result. So the Gloss says: "Good zeal is a fervor of spirit, by which, scorning the fear of death, one is on fire for the defense of the truth. He is consumed by it who takes steps to correct any perversity he sees; and if he cannot, he tolerates it with sadness." (Comm. John, ch. 2, 2.392)

REFLECTION

Following the example of our Lord, we can be zealous for the temple of the Lord in two ways. The first has to do with love of the holy church buildings which are the places in which the Eucharistic sacrifice and worship takes place. Thus, we find a natural desire to design churches with high architectural style as fitting places for divine worship. Moreover, we desire to adorn our churches with beautiful art so that, just as the structure should lift the soul to God, so too, the decorative elements and works of art illustrate the divine mysteries upon which we are to meditate. Thus, our minds are transformed inwardly, so that our outward actions may correspond to the precepts of charity.

The second way to be zealous has to do with the temple of the Holy Spirit, our bodies and souls. Our Lord became angry because the Temple was being abused. It was meant for the worship of God, but had become a marketplace, a place where attention was turned away from God and toward lower values. If zeal for the Lord's house is to consume us, we must become aware of the proper use of our bodies and souls as well as guard against any abuse whatsoever. Thus, we adorn our bodies with modesty and our souls with virtue. We carry ourselves in a manner worthy of the name of Christian, never allowing anything degrading to besmirch our human and Christian dignity. Such zeal not only brings about the fulfillment of the laws of God, but does so in a way which is contrary to any legalism, but sets us free to live in the freedom of the children of God. As a result, even our very bearing is a testimony to the truth of the Catholic faith.

PRAYER

Lord Jesus Christ, you taught us to love your Father's house and to care for the temple that is our body by being raised from the dead bodily in order to lead us into the true worship of God. Inspire us to persevere in our Lenten practices to build up your living body, the Church, by all that we do and say and think with our own bodies and souls. Amen.

GOSPEL

Some people told Jesus about the Galileans whose blood Pilate had mingled with the blood of their sacrifices. Jesus said to them in reply, "Do you think that because these Galileans suffered in this way they were greater sinners than all other Galileans? By no means! But I tell you, if you do not repent, you will all perish as they did! Or those eighteen people who were killed when the tower at Siloam fell on them – do you think they were more guilty than everyone else who lived in Jerusalem? By no means! But I tell you, if you do not repent, you will all perish as they did!"

And he told them this parable: "There once was a person who had a fig tree planted in his orchard, and when he came in search of fruit on it but found none, he said to the gardener, 'For three years now I have come in search of fruit on this fig tree but have found none. So cut it down. Why should it exhaust the soil?' He said to him in reply, 'Sir, leave it for this year also, and I shall cultivate the ground around it and fertilize it; it may bear fruit in the future. If not you can cut it down.'"

LUKE 13: 1-9

ST. THOMAS AQUINAS

God acts mercifully, certainly not by doing something against his justice, but by working above his justice. Take this illustration: a man is owed a hundred, and you give him two hundred from your own pocket; there is no injustice in the deal, and you are being tenderhearted and openhanded. So it is when someone forgives an offence committed against him. For in forgiving the offence he is giving a gift. Hence St. Paul calls forgiving a giving, "Forgiving one another as God in Christ forgave you" (Eph 4:33). Clearly mercy does not take justice away, but is in a sense its fullness. Thus St. James says, "Mercy triumphs over judgment" (2:13). (*ST* Ia, q. 21, a. 3, ad 2 [G modified])

REFLECTION

Not everything evil that befalls a person is a punishment for sin. Our Lord makes this clear when he teaches that the catastrophe that befell certain Galileans was not on account of their guilt. Jesus uses the occasion, however, to teach that we must all reform lest we come to a bad end on the Day of Judgment. As it is with the fig tree that produced no fruit, so it will be with each one of us. Fortunately for the fig tree in the parable, and ourselves, we who are reading this have been given one more chance to bear good fruit. Implicit in this opportunity for change is the knowledge that such delays do not go on forever; the choice for reform is ours and we must not put off our conversion even one moment longer.

Underneath these accounts of the Galileans and the fig tree is the justice and mercy of God. God's patience, his delay in calling us to account for ourselves, is not a defect in his justice, as St. Thomas points out. In this beautiful explanation of mercy, we find that mercy supersedes divine justice. Far from being some kind of emotion or sentiment in God by which he feels sorry for us, his mercy is a perfection by which he gives of himself what is due by justice, and then some. The overabundance is, of course, immeasurable, particularly in the case of the Son becoming man in order to suffer and die in our stead.

When we meditate on such generous mercy of God, we are moved more by awe and reverence than by fear and dread to change our ways for the better. For it is not that God takes delight in our destruction (as Christ points out in the example of the Galileans); rather he desires that we live. Else why would he take the trouble to send his Son to bear our burdens and sins? Why would God allow himself to suffer such ignominious punishments in his own body and soul, if not for love of us, and a desire to overpay the demands of justice when we who owe an immeasurable debt had not a cent to our name?

PRAYER

Father in heaven, your mercy far outweighs the demands of justice. Teach us to see sin for what it is: the undoing of ourselves, the frustration of our true happiness. Enlighten our minds that we may see the depths of your mercy and ever praise the glories of your love each day of our lives and for eternity, in the union of Christ your Son, and the Holy Spirit. Amen.

GOSPEL

JESUS SAID TO THE PEOPLE IN THE SYNAGOGUE AT NAZARETH:

"Amen, I say to you, no prophet is accepted in his own native place. Indeed, I tell you, there were many widows in Israel in the days of Elijah when the sky was closed for three and a half years and a severe famine spread over the entire land. It was to none of these that Elijah was sent, but only to a widow in Zarephath in the land of Sidon. Again, there were many lepers in Israel during the time of Elisha the prophet; yet not one of them was cleansed, but only Naaman the Syrian." When the people in the synagogue heard this, they were all filled with fury. They rose up, drove him out of the town, and led him to the brow of the hill on which their town had been built, to hurl him down headlong. But he passed through the midst of them and went away.

LUKE 4: 24-30

ST. THOMAS AQUINAS

Concerning whether Christ should have preached without offending his audience, Aquinas responds: A man ought so to avoid giving offence, that he is not by improper word or deed the occasion of anyone's downfall. "But if scandal arise from the truth, the scandal should be sustained rather than the truth be relinquished," as [St.] Gregory says. (ST IIIa, q. 42, a. 2, ad 1 [G])

REFLECTION

Ironically, it is often those who know us well who tend to find fault with us when we try to speak a word of change or correction, or even when we simply seek to live more virtuously. They know our past faults and failings and it may appear to them that our attempts to live the converted life amount to little more than counterfeit spirituality.

Other times, they may take our words and actions as an attack on their chosen way of life. Yet such could never be the case with Christ and those who knew him, and so we find ourselves amazed by the hardheartedness that would try even to throw him over the cliff. Indeed, as St. Thomas points out, Christ did avoid giving offence by "improper word or deed" lest he be the downfall of any person, historically and in the present moment. No greater proof of this can be found than in his crucifixion and death for our sake.

On the other hand, he is the one who is most able to speak the truth for he is truth incarnate. Thus, neither the people to whom he preached, nor we, have any reason to be scandalized by his teaching and correction. Rather, since he has proved himself by dying and rising for us, we can trust that our Good Shepherd will speak just the right word with the tone of voice each one of us needs in any particular moment—be it a word of encouragement or healing, or even correction. God always wants only what is best for each person. Let us then not run from the truth Christ speaks to each one individually. When Aquinas says that we should sustain the scandal rather than lose the truth, he means that we should be willing to weather whatever shortlived sting a word of reproof from Christ might bring. The pain is as nothing compared to the freedom and life the word of Christ brings to us. After all, "the truth will make you free" (John 8:32).

PRAYER

Lord God, grant me the grace of humble docility to every one of your words. Make me recall that even your correction is an encouragement, for you desire, not that I be led astray on the false path which leads to death, but that I be made whole and live with you for all eternity. Speak your word to me in prayer and through those whom you have placed in my life, and open my ears that I may hear and obey. Amen.

GOSPEL

Peter approached Jesus and asked him, "Lord, if my brother sins against me, how often must I forgive him? As many as seven times?" Jesus answered, "I say to you, not seven times but seventy-seven times. That is why the Kingdom of heaven may be likened to a king who decided to settle accounts with his servants. When he began the accounting, a debtor was brought before him who owed him a huge amount. Since he had no way of paying it back, his master ordered him to be sold, along with his wife, his children, and all his property, in payment of the debt. At that, the servant fell down, did him homage, and said, 'Be patient with me, and I will pay you back in full.' Moved with compassion the master of that servant let him go and forgave him the loan. When that servant had left, he found one of his fellow servants who owed him a much smaller amount. He seized him and started to choke him, demanding, 'Pay back what you owe.' Falling to his knees, his fellow servant begged him, 'Be patient with me, and I will pay you back.' But he refused. Instead, he had him put in prison until he paid back the debt. Now when his fellow servants saw what had happened, they were deeply disturbed, and went to their master and reported the whole affair. His master summoned him and said to him, 'You wicked servant! I forgave you your entire debt because you begged me to. Should you not have had pity on your fellow servant, as I had pity on you?' Then in anger his master handed him over to the torturers until he should pay back the whole debt. So will my heavenly Father do to you, unless each of you forgives your brother from your heart."

MATTHEW 18: 21-35

ST. THOMAS AQUINAS

[T]he mercy of God grants pardon to sinners through penance is without any limits. Hence it is written, "Immense and unsearchable is the mercy of thy promise, above the sins of men" (Prayer of Manasses, v. 6). Hence it is manifest that Penance can be administered many times. (ST IIIa, q. 84, a. 10, corpus [G])

REFLECTION

Forgiving others is a key component of the teaching of Jesus and takes a central role in the season of Lent, especially for us who are seeking God's forgiveness. While we may be scandalized by the behavior of the servant whose large debt was cancelled but who throttled his peer who owed him a mere fraction, we must admit that at one time or another we have behaved similarly. Are we equally scandalized by our own unforgiving hearts?

Fortunately for us, as it is the case with every grace, God does not wait for us to act first and then reward us. Always he takes the initiative. We love because he first loved us. And so, we forgive because he first forgives us, as did the king in the parable. We may be slow to learn the lesson to give to others as we have received, and so, as St. Thomas points out, God continues to pardon us, particularly through the sacrament of penance, which we are able to receive frequently.

The sacrament of penance is a generous outpouring of God's mercy on us, especially for those who have committed mortal sins after baptism. An essential element to deep spiritual growth is to make frequent use of the sacrament of penance. By regularly confessing our sins in this sacrament we are healed of the roots of those sins and are strengthened by the sacramental grace to grow in virtue and holiness. We become more like our Father as we allow the grace of penance to mold us into his image. We even begin to *desire* to forgive others and recognize the futility of seeking forgiveness without first being willing to forgive. The act of forgiving others is no longer bewildering but becomes a part of normal Christian living because we are no longer relying on our own power. We operate with supernatural gifts.

PRAYER

Lord Jesus Christ, you have taught us to forgive as we have been forgiven; and you give the grace to do what you have commanded. Deepen in us the desire for and the use of frequent sacramental confession so that we may have the grace not only of being forgiven but to forgive with your divine power all others who have wronged us in any way. Amen.

GOSPEL

JESUS SAID TO HIS DISCIPLES:

"Do not think that I have come to abolish the law or the prophets. I have come not to abolish but to fulfill. Amen, I say to you, until heaven and earth pass away, not the smallest letter or the smallest part of a letter will pass from the law, until all things have taken place. Therefore, whoever breaks one of the least of these commandments and teaches others to do so will be called least in the Kingdom of heaven. But whoever obeys and teaches these commandments will be called greatest in the Kingdom of heaven."

MATTHEW 5: 17-19

ST. THOMAS AQUINAS

The words, "who art in heaven" [of the Lord's Prayer] . . . serves as a preparation for him who utters the prayer, for, as it is said: "Before prayer prepare your soul" (Sir. 18:23). Thus, "in heaven" is understood for the glory of heaven: "For your reward is very great in heaven" (Matt 5:12). And this preparation ought to be in the form of an imitation of heavenly things, since the son ought to imitate his father: "Therefore, as we have borne the image of the earthly, let us bear also the image of the heavenly" (1 Cor 15:49). So also this preparation ought to be through contemplation of heavenly things, because men are wont to direct their thoughts to where they have a Father and others whom they love, as it is written: "For where your treasure is, there is your heart also" (Matt 6:21). The Apostle [Paul] wrote: "Our conversation is in heaven" (Phil. 3:20). Likewise, we prepare through attention to heavenly things, so that we may then seek only spiritual things from Him who is in heaven: "Seek things that are above, where Christ is" (Col. 3:1). (Catechetical Instructions: The Lord's Prayer [modified])

REFLECTION

Notice that our Lord does not avoid showing us how to be great in heaven. Rather, he tells us precisely who shall be great in that eternal kingdom: those who obey the commandments of God and teach others to do the same. On the other hand, disregard for the divine ordering has dire consequences.

We must beware lest we fall into the trap of thinking that Christ's instructions for attaining heaven involve only scrupulous obedience or human effort that is more akin to Pharisaism. St. Thomas shows us the way to avoid these snares as we seek heaven. He teaches that we should keep our eyes on our great reward in heaven, not as something we earn on our own, but the result of imitating our Father and his goodness. Immediately we notice that we must take our focus off ourselves and put it on God. It is not so much a matter of *earning* heaven as attaining the goal, which is union with the Father whom we love and after whom we pattern all our actions.

Moreover, St. Thomas makes clear the very basic, but often overlooked, lesson that we should think about heaven, contemplate it, and love it. Just as I might think about the place to which I will travel on a lengthy and fun vacation, imagining the surroundings and people there as well as looking forward to sharing in the good food and drink, more should I anticipate and hope for heaven. We should begin to put all our stock in heaven, with the holy hope of attaining it. It is helpful to think of our loved ones whom we want to see in heaven, and all the saints who await us; but more so, we must cultivate the desire to see God face to face, resting in his love for all time. In this way, we will begin to see that even the seemingly small or least elements of God's law have great meaning and purpose. We will desire to be obedient not out of fear or scrupulosity but on account of the reverence we have for our Father and his ordering of the universe.

PRAYER

Father in heaven, you have placed in us the desire for happiness which can only be fulfilled in gazing upon your face in heaven. Help us to love heaven, and bring our holy desires to fruition, causing us to live now in perfect obedience as we anticipate your bringing us into your holy presence for all eternity. Amen.

GOSPEL

Jesus was driving out a demon that was mute, and when the demon had gone out, the mute man spoke and the crowds were amazed. Some of them said, "By the power of Beelzebul, the prince of demons, he drives out demons." Others, to test him, asked him for a sign from heaven. But he knew their thoughts and said to them, "Every kingdom divided against itself will be laid waste and house will fall against house. And if Satan is divided against himself, how will his kingdom stand? For you say that it is by Beelzebul that I drive out demons. If I, then, drive out demons by Beelzebul, by whom do your own people drive them out? Therefore they will be your judges. But if it is by the finger of God that I drive out demons, then the Kingdom of God has come upon you. When a strong man fully armed guards his palace, his possessions are safe. But when one stronger than he attacks and overcomes him, he takes away the armor on which he relied and distributes the spoils. Whoever is not with me is against me, and whoever does not gather with me scatters."

LUKE 11: 14-23

ST. THOMAS AQUINAS

[St.] Gregory says, "Obedience rightly is rated above sacrifice, for in sacrifice the flesh of another being is offered; in obedience, one's own will." For this reason, as well, any of the acts of other virtues stand before God as meritorious because they are done out of obedience to his will. Even suffering martyrdom or distributing one's goods to the poor would no more be meritorious if not done in fulfillment of God's will, i.e., as acts of obedience, than if they were done without charity, which in turn cannot exist without obedience. The First Letter of John states, "He who says that he knows him and keeps not his commands is a liar. . . . But he that keeps his word in him in very deed the charity of God is perfected" (1 John 2:4). This is so because friendship makes friends one in what they will and in

what they reject. (ST IIa–IIae, q. 104, a. 3 [G modified])

REFLECTION

Oddly enough, while the demon in the gospel was obedient to Jesus, some of Christ's own people were not, going so far as to accuse him of acting by evil powers. It seems that these people trusted more in themselves, and in their own deeds, rather than in the deeds of the Son of God who came to cast down the kingdom of Satan so that we might enter the Kingdom of God.

However, Christ does not desire mere obedience to a set of rules; this kind of obedience is no better than the self-reliant sacrifices of the scribes and Pharisees of old. Rather, Christ has come to us in order to raise us up in friendship with God, that we might be one in mind in willing the good and rejecting all evil. Virtuous friends desire the good and the true. We can even say that friendship entails obedience to another, not oppressive slavery to the will of another, but a union of minds and hearts. Thus, as St. Thomas teaches, is charity perfected in us, that we want the good that God desires. We act freely in these choices, even if our freedom is helped by divine grace issuing from the very being of our Divine Friend such that we more fully use our freedom for perfection and flourishing. When we rightly understand obedience in this light, we need not worry about our Lord's admonition that "whoever is not with me is against me, and whoever does not gather with me scatters," for we shall walk steadfastly with him as he leads us to live intimately with him now and in eternity.

PRAYER

Lord Jesus, my Master, teach me the true meaning of love and obedience that I may live more and more freely in you and for you. Grant that I may more perfectly contemplate your obedient life of sacrifice so that I may learn how to unite my own sacrifices with yours, living not for myself but for you, my truest Friend, and for all those you have given me to love and obey. Amen.

GOSPEL

One of the scribes came to Jesus and asked him, "Which is the first of all the commandments?" Jesus replied, "The first is this: *Hear, O Israel! The Lord our God is Lord alone! You shall love the Lord your God with all your heart, with all your soul, with all your mind, and with all your strength.* The second is this: *You shall love your neighbor as yourself.* There is no other commandment greater than these." The scribe said to him, "Well said, teacher. You are right in saying, *He is One and there is no other than he.* And *to love him with all your heart, with all your understanding, with all your strength, and to love your neighbor as yourself* is worth more than all burnt offerings and sacrifices." And when Jesus saw that he answered with understanding, he said to him, "You are not far from the Kingdom of God." And no one dared to ask him any more questions.

MARK 12: 28-34

ST. THOMAS AQUINAS

We must realize that love is an act of the will signified here by the word "heart." Now just as the bodily heart is the principle of all bodily movements so the will is the principle of all spiritual movements, and most of all when its intent is on the last end, which is the object of charity. Now there are three springs of action which are moved by the will: the intellect, signified by "mind"; the lower appetitive power, signified by "soul"; and the external executive power signified by "strength," or "power" or "might." So now when we are told to love God what are we commanded? That our full intent be on God, "with all your heart"; that our intellect be subject to God, "with all your mind"; that our appetite be ruled by God, "with all your soul"; and that our exterior action be obedient to God, with all your strength or power or might. (ST IIa–IIae, q. 44, a. 5 [G])

REFLECTION

All are called to conversion, that is, deeper love of God, especially during this season of Lent. Some are converting afresh to Christianity; others are Christians whose hearts have grown lukewarm, or even cold; still others live a deeply religious life but nevertheless need an even greater fire burning away the dross of the sins of the past. Conversion principally is a turning of the heart in love to God, not the mere following of precepts and commands in some external way.

We should not think that we must somehow stir divine love in our hearts on our own. This act of the will set on our last end which is union with God does not proceed first from ourselves nor by our effort. It is all a sheer gift from God who has first loved us. As the aphorism goes, God does not love us because we are good; we are good because God loves us. In other words, it is not that we do something to earn initial divine love. Rather, God's love makes us good and moves us to love him in return, and to love ourselves in right order, and to love our neighbor as God loves. The love we lack is available superabundantly from God and is infused into our souls by the Holy Spirit.

This gift of divine love liberates us from the disordered turning-in on ourselves. Whereas the disordered love of self and others seeks primarily to gain other persons or things, to own them, divine love is self-giving. This is why we need conversion. Conversion is not essentially the giving up of sin. Conversion is the transformation of self-directed love to real and outward love, sacrificial love. It is sacrificial because it is the ardent burning up of self-interest for the sake of the other. It is almost miraculous because it is a fire that grows hotter and brighter, because its source, its fuel, is the infinite Godhead.

Remember that God cannot command the impossible. When he commands that we love with all our heart, soul, mind and strength, it is because he works this love in us, with us.

PRAYER

Divine Spirit of Love, enflame my heart anew. Make me all ablaze with the love that comes from Christ's passion. Recreate my heart to be a burning furnace of charity, like the Heart of Jesus, seeking to love God the Father for himself and my neighbor as myself. Grant me freedom from self-interest that I may be an image of your complete, ever-sacrificing love. Amen.

GOSPEL

Jesus addressed this parable to those who were convinced of their own righteousness and despised everyone else. "Two people went up to the temple area to pray; one was a Pharisee and the other was a tax collector. The Pharisee took up his position and spoke this prayer to himself, 'O God, I thank you that I am not like the rest of humanity—greedy, dishonest, adulterous—or even like this tax collector. I fast twice a week, and I pay tithes on my whole income.' But the tax collector stood off at a distance and would not even raise his eyes to heaven but beat his breast and prayed, 'O God, be merciful to me a sinner.' I tell you, the latter went home justified, not the former; for everyone who exalts himself will be humbled, and the one who humbles himself will be exalted."

LUKE 18: 9-14

ST. THOMAS AQUINAS

[M]editation is the cause of devotion since through meditation man conceives the idea of giving himself to God. A man forms this idea in one of two ways. The first is by considering the divine goodness and kindness, which leads to the thought expressed in the Psalms, "It is good for me to cling to my God, to put my hope in the Lord" (Ps 82:28). Considerations of this type awaken love which is the proximate cause of devotion. The second way is by considering man's weaknesses, which leads to the realization that man must depend upon God. Hence the Psalmist says, "I lift up my eyes to the mountains, whence help shall come to me; my help is from the Lord, who made heaven and earth" (120:1). Consideration of man's weaknesses leads a man to submit to God since it banishes presumption which leads man to trust in his own strength. (ST IIa–IIae, q. 82, a. 3 [G])

119

REFLECTION

St. Thomas, shortly after the passage above, says that people of learning or other qualities of greatness make such individuals tend to trust themselves rather than surrendering themselves to God (*ST* IIa–IIae, q. 82, a. 3, ad 3 [G]). We see this particularly in the case of the gospel for today where the Pharisee, with prominent display in the temple, lauds himself for his supposed virtue, all the while avoiding true contact with God. On the other hand, the tax collector stays in the back of the temple, begging divine mercy. This one, St. Thomas teaches, aware of his sins and weaknesses, has come to know that he has nothing upon which to depend except God himself. Thus he truly surrenders to God and, as our Lord says, was justified. Such is the lesson for us to put aside our cleverness so that nothing stands in the way of giving ourselves to God. We begin by humbling ourselves, begging mercy and forgiveness each day.

During Lent we are urged to pray more. This means making time in our lives for meditation. Meditation is the prayer by which we ponder God and the things of God. It involves ruminating over the words of Sacred Scripture, delving into the events and mysteries of the life of Christ and the deeds of God, pondering the myriad graces we have been given throughout our lives, thinking about the effects the sacraments have had on us, and so forth. It is a time not for making petitions (except for the petition to be more open to the workings of the Holy Spirit) but for speaking with God heart to heart and patiently waiting to hear the words he wants to speak to us. Such prayer then becomes more and more the center of our lives and insures that God, not we, will occupy center stage and justify us.

PRAYER

Lord God, in your mercy send your Holy Spirit to enlighten my mind to know my weaknesses and sins more clearly so that I may grow in repentance each day of my life. Grant me the grace to meditate on the wonders of your handiwork in creation and your work of re-creating the world through the passion, death, and resurrection of Christ your Son. Open my ears that I may hear your every word and obey your directions so that I may love you with all my being. Amen.

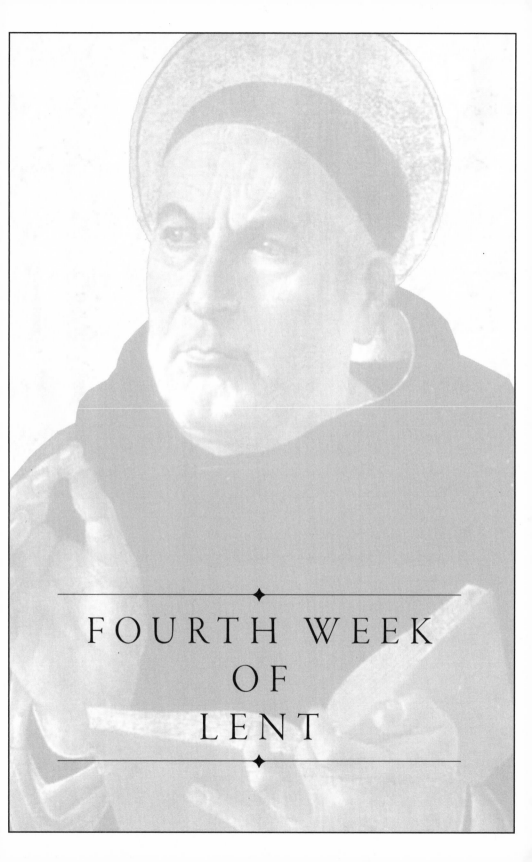

FOURTH WEEK
OF
LENT

GOSPEL

As Jesus passed by he saw a man blind from birth. His disciples asked him, "Rabbi, who sinned, this man or his parents, that he was born blind?" Jesus answered, "Neither he nor his parents sinned; it is so that the works of God might be made visible through him. We have to do the works of the one who sent me while it is day. Night is coming when no one can work. While I am in the world, I am the light of the world." When he had said this, he spat on the ground and made clay with the saliva, and smeared the clay on his eyes, and said to him, "Go wash in the Pool of Siloam" —which means Sent—. So he went and washed, and came back able to see.

His neighbors and those who had seen him earlier as a beggar said, "Isn't this the one who used to sit and beg?" Some said, "It is," but others said, "No, he just looks like him." He said, "I am." So they said to him, "How were your eyes opened?" He replied, "The man called Jesus made clay and anointed my eyes and told me, 'Go to Siloam and wash.' So I went there and washed and was able to see." And they said to him, "Where is he?" He said, "I don't know."

They brought the one who was once blind to the Pharisees. Now Jesus had made clay and opened his eyes on a sabbath. So then the Pharisees also asked him how he was able to see. He said to them, "He put clay on my eyes, and I washed, and now I can see." So some of the Pharisees said, "This man is not from God, because he does not keep the sabbath." But others said, "How can a sinful man do such signs?" And there was a division among them. So they said to the blind man again, "What do you have to say about him, since he opened your eyes?" He said, "He is a prophet."

Now the Jews did not believe that he had been blind and gained his sight until they summoned the parents of the one who had gained his sight. They asked them, "Is this your son, who you say was born blind? How does he now see?" His parents answered and said, "We know that this is our son and that he was born blind. We do not know how he sees now, nor do we know who opened his eyes. Ask him, he is of age; he can speak for himself." His parents said this because they were afraid of the Jews, for the Jews had already agreed that if anyone acknowledged him as the Christ, he would be expelled from the synagogue. For this reason his parents said, "He is of age; question him."

So a second time they called the man who had been blind and said to him, "Give God the praise! We know that this man is a sinner." He replied, "If he is a sinner, I do not know. One thing I do know is that I was blind and now I see." So they said to him, "What did he do to you? How did he open your eyes?" He answered them, "I told you already and you did not listen. Why do you want to hear it again? Do you want to become his disciples, too?" They ridiculed him and said, "You are that man's disciple; we are disciples of Moses! We know that God spoke to Moses, but we do not know where this one is from." The man answered and said to them, "This is what is so amazing, that you do not know where he is from, yet he opened my eyes. We know that God does not listen to sinners, but if one is devout and does his will, he listens to him. It is unheard of that anyone ever opened the eyes of a person born blind. If this man were not from God, he would not be able to do anything." They answered and said to him, "You were born totally in sin, and are you trying to teach us?" Then they threw him out.

When Jesus heard that they had thrown him out, he found him and said, "Do you believe in the Son of Man?" He answered and said, "Who is he, sir, that I may believe in him?" Jesus said to him, "You have seen him, the one speaking with you is he." He said, "I do believe, Lord," and he worshiped him. Then Jesus said, "I came into this world for judgment, so that those who do not see might see, and those who do see might become blind."

> Some of the Pharisees who were with him heard this and said to him, "Surely we are not also blind, are we?" Jesus said to them, "If you were blind, you would have no sin; but now you are saying, 'We see,' so your sin remains."
>
> JOHN 9: 1-41
>
> Shorter form: JOHN 9:1, 6-9, 13-17, 34-38
>
> Longer form may be optionally read on any day in the fourth week of Lent

ST. THOMAS AQUINAS

Augustine gives the mystical and allegorical explanation. He says that the spittle, which is saliva that descends from the head, signifies the Word of God, who proceeds from the Father, the head of all things: "I came forth from the mouth of the Most High" (Sir 24:3). Therefore, the Lord made clay from spittle and the earth when the Word was made flesh. He anointed the eyes of the blind man, that is, of the human race. And the eyes are the eyes of the heart, anointed by faith in the incarnation of Christ. But the blind man did not yet see, because the anointing produced a catechumen, who has faith but has not yet been baptized. So he sends him to the pool of Siloam to wash and receive his sight, i.e., to be baptized, and in baptism to receive full enlightenment. Thus, according to Denis, baptism is an enlightenment: "I will sprinkle clean water upon you, and you shall be clean from all your uncleanness" (Ezek 36:25). And so this Gospel is appropriately read in Lent . . . when those about to be baptized are examined. Nor is it without reason that the Evangelist adds the meaning of the pool, saying, "which means sent," because whoever is baptized must be baptized in Christ, who was sent by the Father: "As many of you as were baptized in Christ have put on Christ" (Gal 3:27). For if Christ had not been sent, none of us would have been freed from sin. (Comm. John, ch. 9, 1.1311)

REFLECTION

Aquinas brings Augustine's insight to bear on this gospel passage. Both the catechumen and the baptized Christian profit by meditating on baptism as an opening of our eyes, a healing of the blindness caused by original sin as well as personal sin.

Christ Jesus tells us that he is the light of the world. Notice that our Lord does not tell us that he is one light among many, or even among a few. He is *the* light. Whatever other lights we have relied on till now are not the real light, but derive whatever faint ray they may shed from him alone. Nevertheless, apart from Christ we walk in darkness. No political party, no earthly leader, no scientific discovery, no human love, can bring us out of our darkness. Even if they seemingly offer some momentary glimmer, they are by nature doomed to be swallowed up in darkness because they are temporal. We need the light that cannot be dimmed or put out. Such is Christ.

St. Thomas notes elsewhere in this commentary that overcoming our blindness is not something we can do on our own. As unseemly as it may appear, Christ makes a paste of dirt and saliva to heal the man's blindness and then tells him to wash in the Pool of Siloam. When man was created, God breathed life into the mud he had fashioned into the first man. Now the Word coming from the mouth of the Father recreates us who had been driven into darkness by the sin of Adam and Eve. We are made to see again, but not just see the world. We see the world for what it is; and we can begin to see, again, the way home to our Father as we make our way on our pilgrimage through this world. We see, too, that all that glitters around us is not necessarily a good light, but may well be nothing more than a fanciful distraction, keeping us from what we should be about.

Do not think that it is enough to be healed of your blindness, that it is enough simply to be baptized and thus be considered a Christian. Vision is given, not so that a person can see only the surface of things around him, but so that he can know the reality behind the visual stimuli. So it is in the Christian life. We are meant to see the truth of this world and the truth of God. We must train our vision, and even learn to see more clearly as we draw closer to the Light of the world. This means that our eyes must adjust to the greater light, so that our vision is ever more penetrating. Such is the life of prayer as we expose our lives to the light of Christ in the sacraments of penance and the Holy Eucharist. God will show us things beyond our imagining, give us insights beyond mere human powers, and ultimately bring us to the vision of himself, an impossibility unless we have been given eyes to behold his glory.

PRAYER

Lord God, deepen within our souls the power of the grace of baptism that our minds may be enlightened with a greater knowledge of you and our wills inflamed with a greater love of you; and grant that we may hasten on our way to your kingdom amid the snares of this world, with your light to guide our feet. Amen.

GOSPEL

JESUS SAID TO NICODEMUS:

"Just as Moses lifted up the serpent in the desert, so must the Son of Man be lifted up, so that everyone who believes in him may have eternal life."

For God so loved the world that he gave his only Son, so that everyone who believes in him might not perish but might have eternal life. For God did not send his Son into the world to condemn the world, but that the world might be saved through him. Whoever believes in him will not be condemned, but whoever does not believe has already been condemned, because he has not believed in the name of the only Son of God. And this is the verdict, that the light came into the world, but people preferred darkness to light, because their works were evil. For everyone who does wicked things hates the light and does not come toward the light, so that his works might not be exposed. But whoever lives the truth comes to the light, so that his works may be clearly seen as done in God.

JOHN 3: 14-21

ST. THOMAS AQUINAS

Now the fruit of Christ's passion is eternal life; hence he says "so that everyone who believes in him," performing good works, "may not be lost, but have eternal life." And this fruit corresponds to the fruit of the symbolic serpent. For whoever looked upon the serpent of bronze was freed from poison and his life was preserved. But he who looks upon the lifted up Son of Man, and believes in the crucified Christ, he is freed from poison and sin: "Whoever believes in me will never die" (John 11:26), and is preserved for eternal life. "These things are written that you may believe . . . and that believing you may have life in his name" (John 20:31). . . .

129

He indicates the immensity of God's love in saying, "have eternal life": for by giving eternal life, he gives himself. For eternal life is nothing else than enjoying God. But to give oneself is a sign of great love: "But God, who is rich in mercy, has brought us to life in Christ" (Eph. 2:5), i.e., he gave us eternal life. (Comm. John ch. 3, 2.475, 3.480)

REFLECTION

Archbishop Augustine DiNoia, O.P.[1] is fond of saying that no one desires anything more than God desires our union with him. God does not need our union with him in order to be happy; he wants our union so that *we* can be happy. This is why he made us in the first place. Yet, he also made us with free will so that our love may be like his: choosing the good.

Sin is the choice against the good, both our good and the good which is God himself. Though the choice for sin has always been ours, God has never abandoned us to the effects of our sin. This is seen, for instance, in the event of the Israelites wandering in the desert, grumbling against God, and suffering the poisonous bites of the serpents in the midst of their stubborn refusal to love God above all else. God commanded Moses to make a bronze serpent and mount it on a pole so that anyone who looked at it would recover. Our own healing comes from Christ himself being lifted up on the cross, so that whoever believes in him will recover, that is, have eternal life.

But what does it mean to believe in Christ? It means, first of all, to assent to his divinity as well as his humanity, that he is the Son whom God sent into our world because God so loved the world. We must respond, for salvation is not an automatic given by claiming to be a Christian. Unlike the Israelites in the desert who only experienced this special healing by looking at the bronze serpent but did not gain eternal life, we more than look on the crucified Christ. He enables us to know and love him in a personal relationship. Notice that he enables

---

1. Formerly the Secretary of the Vatican Congregation for Divine Worship and the Discipline of the Sacraments, and now the Vice-President of the Pontifical Commission *Ecclesia Dei.*

us; the beginning of new life is not something we are able to accomplish on our own.

To believe in Christ means also to dwell in his light, that is, to live according to the truth and to shun the darkness of evil deeds and thoughts. Our works as done in God will be seen, St. John tells us, because we do not fear the light. Our chief work will be to give ourselves entirely to Christ through the life of daily prayer and the sacramental life and the life of virtue. God, who desires our happiness more than we do, is always drawing us to himself with myriad graces. May we respond to such generosity with minds and hearts made for the truth and light and love.

PRAYER

Father in heaven, you have so loved the world that you sent your Son so that we may have eternal life. We rejoice in the gift of Christ, your Son and our light. Grant us a living faith so that we may be transformed by lifting our eyes to the Crucified One in deeper prayer and the sacramental life. May the light of Christ be evident in all our deeds of charity for others. Amen.

GOSPEL

Tax collectors and sinners were all drawing near to listen to Jesus, but the Pharisees and scribes began to complain, saying, "This man welcomes sinners and eats with them." So to them Jesus addressed this parable: "A man had two sons, and the younger son said to his father, 'Father, give me the share of your estate that should come to me.' So the father divided the property between them. After a few days, the younger son collected all his belongings and set off to a distant country where he squandered his inheritance on a life of dissipation. When he had freely spent everything, a severe famine struck that country, and he found himself in dire need. So he hired himself out to one of the local citizens who sent him to his farm to tend the swine. And he longed to eat his fill of the pods on which the swine fed, but nobody gave him any. Coming to his senses he thought, 'How many of my father's hired workers have more than enough food to eat, but here am I, dying from hunger. I shall get up and go to my father and I shall say to him, "Father, I have sinned against heaven and against you. I no longer deserve to be called your son; treat me as you would treat one of your hired workers."' So he got up and went back to his father. While he was still a long way off, his father caught sight of him, and was filled with compassion. He ran to his son, embraced him and kissed him. His son said to him, 'Father, I have sinned against heaven and against you; I no longer deserve to be called your son.' But his father ordered his servants, 'Quickly, bring the finest robe and put it on him; put a ring on his finger and sandals on his feet. Take the fattened calf and slaughter it. Then let us celebrate with a feast, because this son of mine was dead, and has come to life again; he was lost, and has been found.' Then the celebration began. Now the older son had been out in the field and, on his way back, as he neared the house, he heard the sound of music and dancing. He called one of the servants and asked what this might mean. The servant said to him, 'Your brother has returned and your father has slaughtered the fattened calf because he has him back safe and sound.' He became angry, and when he refused to enter the house, his father came out and pleaded with him. He said to his father in reply, 'Look, all these years I served you and not once did I disobey your orders; yet you never gave me even a young goat to feast on with my friends. But when your son returns who swallowed up your property with prostitutes, for him you slaughter the fattened calf.' He said to him, 'My son, you are here with me always; everything I have is yours. But now we must celebrate and rejoice, because your brother was dead and has come to life again; he was lost and has been found.'"

LUKE 15: 1-3, 11-32

ST. THOMAS AQUINAS

Mercy . . . means compassion for another's misery, and so the same thing that makes a man merciful makes him grieve over another's misfortune. But sadness or pain are feelings aroused by evils afflicting a man's own self, and so sadness over another's misfortune is measured by the extent to which we see another's misfortune as our own. Now, in the first place, this can be so because two people are one in their affections, a union which is the fruit of love. For, to one who loves, a friend is but another self, and so he counts his friend's misfortunes as his own and grieves over them in the same way. . . . St. Paul, too, tells us to "rejoice with those that rejoice, weep with those that weep" (Rom. 12:15). [And] it may be so because of a union which is so real and close that the affliction of those near us spreads to us. (ST IIa–IIae, q. 30, a. 2 [G])

REFLECTION

The father of the prodigal son embodies mercy par excellence, going out physically and psychologically to await the return of his more-than-wayward son. The other son and brother of the prodigal, who seems to pride himself on never having done anything seriously wrong, cannot understand his father's mercy; nor does he have any mercy for his brother. Actually, it's not that the older brother had never experienced the shame of waywardness that makes him unmerciful, for we don't know his moral past. We do know that he lacks the feeling of pain, the compassion for his brother's misery as well as the reckoning by which one is grieved, even on an intellectual level, to see someone's tribulation. He has no patience for his errant brother. He is not concerned about his brother's conversion and return home.

Conversion is rarely sudden, but even when it is, it most likely has been after a longish period of selfish straying. Like the father of the parable, God patiently waits for us. The image of the elder brother is helpful to see the *via negativa*, that is, what God is *not*. God is not vengeful and uncaring about us when we have abandoned him. He does not fail to grieve, albeit in a non-emotional way. He does not refuse to celebrate, with all of heaven, the return of the lost one. He is not happy to simply leave us dead in our sin. He does not count the cost, either of what he had already done to give us life, or the price of our re-creation, giving even his Son for us. He does not rail against us nor throw our shame in our faces, when we make some attempt to respond to his grace. We could go on, simply by observing the behavior of the older son who more represents a legalistic approach to sinners than one of humble and self-effacing charity.

The slaughter of the fatted calf for the son can easily be taken as a reference to the lavish banquet God provides for us. Our Father wants us to be at his table; he wants us to be fed with the Body and Blood of his Son, Jesus Christ, and clothed with his splendor and glory. He wants us to know our true identity as his sons and daughters. Moreover, he wants to bring us to our place with him in our eternal home which Christ has already prepared for us. May we have the humility to give in to such a loving and caring Father whose desire for us is greater than any love we could ever imagine. Moreover, may we wholeheartedly desire the conversion of our family and friends.

PRAYER

Lord, draw me close to yourself and teach me your deepest love. Feed me with your Body and Blood that I may become what I consume and be consumed with love of you. Let me not stray from your house, that I may always know who I am in you. Form my heart to be like your own so that I may rejoice to see my loved ones return to you. Amen.

GOSPEL

At that time Jesus left [Samaria] for Galilee. For Jesus himself testified that a prophet has no honor in his native place. When he came into Galilee, the Galileans welcomed him, since they had seen all he had done in Jerusalem at the feast; for they themselves had gone to the feast.

Then he returned to Cana in Galilee, where he had made the water wine. Now there was a royal official whose son was ill in Capernaum. When he heard that Jesus had arrived in Galilee from Judea, he went to him and asked him to come down and heal his son, who was near death. Jesus said to him, "Unless you people see signs and wonders, you will not believe." The royal official said to him, "Sir, come down before my child dies." Jesus said to him, "You may go; your son will live." The man believed what Jesus said to him and left. While the man was on his way back, his slaves met him and told him that his boy would live. He asked them when he began to recover. They told him, "The fever left him yesterday, about one in the afternoon." The father realized that just at that time Jesus had said to him, "Your son will live," and he and his whole household came to believe. Now this was the second sign Jesus did when he came to Galilee from Judea.

JOHN 4: 43-54

ST. THOMAS AQUINAS

The obedience of this official is pointed out in two ways. First, because he believed what Christ said; so he [John] says, "The man took Jesus at his word," that is, "Your son lives." Secondly, because he did obey the order of Christ; so he says, he "started for home," progressing in faith, although not yet fully or soundly, as Origen says. This signifies that we must be justified by faith: "Justified by faith, let us have peace with God, through our Lord Jesus Christ" (Rom 5:1). We also must go and start out by making progress: because he who stands still runs the risk of being unable to preserve the life of grace. For, along the road to God, if we do not go forward we fall back. (Comm. John, ch. 4, 7.690)

REFLECTION

In commenting on the miracle of the son of the royal official of Capernaum, St. Thomas shows the gradual deepening of faith of the official as he moves from his initial request to his persistence and finally to trust. Ultimately, the official is obedient by returning home at our Lord's word: "You may go; your son will live." His prayer was answered, though he could not yet know it by personal observation or experience (or what some might think of as science). He knew in another way: by faith. Both science and faith are aimed at getting to the truth. The man believed Jesus, took him at his word, because God, who is truth, cannot deceive. Only after he had set out on his way back home did his servants come to him to tell him that the boy had recovered. Perhaps the slaves were coming to tell him not to bother Jesus since the boy was well, St. Thomas points out. But the man knew better. In asking the hour of the boy's recovery, he received confirmation that our Lord had worked the miracle. Still, there was no material cause-and-effect proof, and the man could have ascribed the healing to happenstance. Instead, the man's faith was strengthened and his entire household came to believe.

Time and again Christ speaks to us and touches our lives in unmistakable ways. He wants us to trust him so that he can manifest himself to us more frequently and more intimately. It all begins at baptism when all our sin is washed away and the divine life of the Trinity rushes into our souls to bring them to new life, just as the healing power of Christ rushed upon the son of the royal official in the gospel at a precise moment in time. But we, too, must cooperate with this grace of divine adoption and new faith. We must grow, get up and move, make progress in our life with Christ, as indeed the father of the boy did in believing Jesus and setting out for home, and as the boy must have done at the hour of his recovery. There is no standing still in the life of grace. Just as muscles must continually work in order to maintain tone and grow strong, so we must really live in Christ, not just spiritually vegetate. Christ has given us new life, a life of day-by-day, minute-by-minute friendship with God. We have divine life in us empowering us to live differently, to see beyond the limits of the material world, to think as God thinks, and to will as he wills.

To walk, to move about, to grow is nothing less than the life of prayer (including the sacraments) and living the virtues, talking to God and listening to him, just the official did. Prayer and divine worship through the sacraments is not something extraordinary for the Christian, any more than walking or thinking is extraordinary for a healthy person. To be alive in Christ means that the life of prayer is to continually deepen, so that we may be of one mind and heart with God himself.

PRAYER

Lord, I believe in you with all my heart, mind, body, and soul. Yet I want to grow deeper in faith, knowing and loving you more intimately each day, each moment of life. Help me pray more deeply and hear your voice more clearly; grant me the grace of living in you alone. I want each day of my life to be one that brings me closer to my true homeland, life with you in eternity. Amen.

GOSPEL

There was a feast of the Jews, and Jesus went up to Jerusalem. Now there is in Jerusalem at the Sheep Gate a pool called in Hebrew Bethesda, with five porticoes. In these lay a large number of ill, blind, lame, and crippled. One man was there who had been ill for thirty-eight years. When Jesus saw him lying there and knew that he had been ill for a long time, he said to him, "Do you want to be well?" The sick man answered him, "Sir, I have no one to put me into the pool when the water is stirred up; while I am on my way, someone else gets down there before me." Jesus said to him, "Rise, take up your mat, and walk." Immediately the man became well, took up his mat, and walked.

Now that day was a sabbath. So the Jews said to the man who was cured, "It is the sabbath, and it is not lawful for you to carry your mat." He answered them, "The man who made me well told me, 'Take up your mat and walk.'" They asked him, "Who is the man who told you, 'Take it up and walk'?" The man who was healed did not know who it was, for Jesus had slipped away, since there was a crowd there. After this Jesus found him in the temple area and said to him, "Look, you are well; do not sin any more, so that nothing worse may happen to you." The man went and told the Jews that Jesus was the one who had made him well. Therefore, the Jews began to persecute Jesus because he did this on a sabbath.

JOHN 5: 1-16

ST. THOMAS AQUINAS

The Lord commanded both the nature of the man and his will, for both are under the Lord's power. He commanded his nature when he said, "Stand up." This command was not directed to the man's will, for this was not within the power of his will. But it was within the power of his nature, to which the Lord gave the power to stand by his command. He gave two commands to the man's will: "pick up your mat and walk!" The literal meaning for this is that these two things were commanded in order to show that the man had been restored to perfect health. For in all his miracles the Lord produced a perfect work, according to what was best in the nature of each case: "The works of God are perfect" (Deut 32:4). Now this man was lacking two things: first his own energy, since he could not stand up by himself, thus our Lord found him lying by the pool. Secondly, he lacked the help of others; so he said, "I have no one." So our Lord, in order that this man might recognize his perfect health, ordered him who could not help himself to pick up his mat, and him who could not walk to walk. (Comm. John, ch. 5, 1.716)

REFLECTION

The first reading for Mass today concerns Ezekiel's vision of the water flowing from the side of the Temple. Taken together with the gospel reference to the Bethesda pool, our thoughts go easily to the sacrament of baptism. The waters of baptism originate from the side of Christ crucified when he was pierced with a lance after he had died, healing us of the deadening effects of sin. The man in the gospel does not plunge into the waters of the pool, but it is nonetheless by Christ's power that he is cured.

It is important for us to reflect on the restorative and perfective powers of baptism. Before baptism, the soul is spiritually lifeless, dead. We might think of the paralyzed limbs of the man in the gospel. He has legs but they are of no avail. He could not so much as get himself into the waters of the pool in order to be healed. So it is with us before baptism. We are completely reliant on Christ to give us the new life of the Spirit, to infuse divine power into us which raises us to new life and continues the work of perfection as we are daily transformed to share in the image of the perfect man, Christ Jesus. No power of our own can work this miracle, but it is easy for our Lord. He has already commanded that baptism have such a healing effect, and his Word penetrates to the depth of one's soul. When the waters of baptism touch us, the divine life of the Trinity restores the image of God in us, by which we know and love God in a new way. Then, by the command of Christ to follow him, to walk with him, the graces of our baptism continue to work, by which we worship the Father in Christ through the Holy Spirit dwelling in us.

Think often of the day of your baptism. Consider the profound effects of this sacrament of new life. By it you were inserted into Christ and the life of the Trinity is now alive in you. No moment of the rest of your life can ever be the same, because once you lay helpless, and now you walk. Once you had no one to give you the ability to walk through life and now you can race to heaven. Once you did not understand life and now Life itself dwells in you. Once you were fated to die apart from Christ and now you will live forever in his company.

PRAYER

Lord, I praise you for the gift of your watchful eye, mercifully regarding my wounds and need for your life and grace. I give you thanks for coming to my aid and for setting me on the path to eternal life. May your word of life permeate my soul that I may praise you more profoundly each day, and live fully the divine life you have given me. Amen.

GOSPEL

Jesus answered the Jews: "My Father is at work until now, so I am at work." For this reason they tried all the more to kill him, because he not only broke the sabbath but he also called God his own father, making himself equal to God.

Jesus answered and said to them, "Amen, amen, I say to you, the Son cannot do anything on his own, but only what he sees the Father doing; for what he does, the Son will do also. For the Father loves the Son and shows him everything that he himself does, and he will show him greater works than these, so that you may be amazed. For just as the Father raises the dead and gives life, so also does the Son give life to whomever he wishes. Nor does the Father judge anyone, but he has given all judgment to the Son, so that all may honor the Son just as they honor the Father. Whoever does not honor the Son does not honor the Father who sent him. Amen, amen, I say to you, whoever hears my word and believes in the one who sent me has eternal life and will not come to condemnation, but has passed from death to life. Amen, amen, I say to you, the hour is coming and is now here when the dead will hear the voice of the Son of God, and those who hear will live. For just as the Father has life in himself, so also he gave to the Son the possession of life in himself. And he gave him power to exercise judgment, because he is the Son of Man. Do not be amazed at this, because the hour is coming in which all who are in the tombs will hear his voice and will come out, those who have done good deeds to the resurrection of life, but those who have done wicked deeds to the resurrection of condemnation.

"I cannot do anything on my own; I judge as I hear, and my judgment is just, because I do not seek my own will but the will of the one who sent me."

JOHN 5: 17-30

ST. THOMAS AQUINAS

When he says, "and my judgment is just," he shows the justness of his judgment. For he had said: "Those who have done well will come forth to a resurrection of life." But some might say: Will he be partial and uneven when he punishes and rewards? So he answers: No, saying: "my judgment is just;" and the reason is "because I am not seeking my own will, but the will of him who sent me." For there are two wills in our Lord Jesus Christ: one is a divine will, which is the same as the will of the Father; the other is a human will, which is proper to himself, just as it is proper to him to be a man. A human will is borne to its own good; but in Christ it was ruled and regulated by right reason, so that it would always be conformed in all things to the divine will. (Comm. John, ch. 5, 5.796)

REFLECTION

There was never a question of Christ's human will (part of his human nature) being set against his divine will, which is the will of his Father. His will has always been in perfect conformity with the Father's because he and the Father are one in divinity. Nor was it onerous for Jesus to conform his human will to the divine will, as we sometimes experience. St. Thomas gives us the reason why there is no tension: Christ's intellect was properly ordered to the truth, and therefore to the good. This is to say that all the thoughts of Jesus Christ were set only on the good and the true. To know the good is to choose it. Thus, his will was always in agreement with the will of the Father, for the Father is the source of all goodness and truth.

We, on the other hand, often experience the fractiousness of minds and wills not in accord with goodness and truth. Our sins are the result of choosing what is only an apparent good, over against what is truly good. Perhaps we are attracted by the gleam of the forbidden fruit and decide not to waste time considering its real worth before choosing to have it. Such is the trouble with wealth, or even time, to take two examples. There is always more to be taken for oneself; never mind that someone else may need a part of it. I want to keep it for myself, regardless of my brother's need for some part of it. Thus, the sin begins. I push others away in my pursuit of this thing I desire more for myself. And the pushing away of others takes a myriad of forms.

The only way to be happy and flourish as a human being is to have a mind conformed to the truth and a will that chooses the true good that the mind sees. We need Christ for this. We need him not merely as an example of the perfect man whose will is perfectly conformed to the will of the Father, but we need him *in* us, giving us the power to be interiorly transformed to know and will the good as it really is.

The judgment about which the gospel speaks is not a matter of the computation of our good deeds in proportion to our sins. It is a matter of having minds and wills conformed to the truth as it is found in God, and this is why Christ is the one to judge us, for he is the Son perfectly conformed to the Father.

PRAYER

Lord, in your mercy grant me the grace of seeing and judging reality as you have created it, of knowing the truly good and choosing only what is in accord with your holy will. Show me the places in my life that are not yet in unity with your mind and will and help me to change all that needs to change in my life, moment by moment, so that I may not fear the Day of Judgment but may live in happiness with you. Amen.

GOSPEL

JESUS SAID TO THE JEWS:

"If I testify on my own behalf, my testimony is not true. But there is another who testifies on my behalf, and I know that the testimony he gives on my behalf is true. You sent emissaries to John, and he testified to the truth. I do not accept human testimony, but I say this so that you may be saved. He was a burning and shining lamp, and for a while you were content to rejoice in his light. But I have testimony greater than John's. The works that the Father gave me to accomplish, these works that I perform testify on my behalf that the Father has sent me. Moreover, the Father who sent me has testified on my behalf. But you have never heard his voice nor seen his form, and you do not have his word remaining in you, because you do not believe in the one whom he has sent. You search the Scriptures, because you think you have eternal life through them; even they testify on my behalf. But you do not want to come to me to have life.

"I do not accept human praise; moreover, I know that you do not have the love of God in you. I came in the name of my Father, but you do not accept me; yet if another comes in his own name, you will accept him. How can you believe, when you accept praise from one another and do not seek the praise that comes from the only God? Do not think that I will accuse you before the Father: the one who will accuse you is Moses, in whom you have placed your hope. For if you had believed Moses, you would have believed me, because he wrote about me. But if you do not believe his writings, how will you believe my words?"

JOHN 5: 31-47

ST. THOMAS AQUINAS

The fruit which you think you have in the Scriptures, that is, eternal life, you will not be able to obtain, because in not believing the testimonies of the Scriptures about me, "you are unwilling to come to me," i.e., you do not wish to believe in me, in whom the fruit of these Scriptures exists, "in order to possess that life" in me, the life which I give to those who believe in me: "I give them eternal life" (John 10:28); "Wisdom infuses life into her children" (Sir 4:12); "He who finds me will find life, and will have salvation from the Lord" (Prov 8:35). (Comm. John, ch. 5, 6.824)

REFLECTION

The Old Testament is the preparation for the New Testament and the light in which the Old Testament must always be read. Everything that is revealed there is for our salvation which culminates in Christ. One difficulty that our Lord addresses in today's gospel passage is that many of the Jewish leaders trusted more in their arbitrary interpretation of the Scriptures. Worse yet, these interpretations were often the fruit of mere personal opinion. The result was that they composed law upon law regulating the smallest details of life and they missed the message of the Scriptures. That is why Christ castigates them for accepting praise from each other rather than seeking God's approval which would come from properly understanding the teaching of Moses.

The safeguard that Christ gives us against falling into the same snare as the Jewish leaders is the Magisterium (the teaching responsibility of the bishops and the pope) of the Catholic Church. The Magisterium is the gift to us to be sure that we hear the living voice of God so that we can correctly understand Divine Revelation. Christ continues to speak to his Church through the Magisterium and Sacred Tradition precisely so that we may properly understand the message of the Bible. We have to be willing to come to Christ and listen to him as he himself interprets for us the meaning of the Scriptures. Thus our belief will be rooted in indubitable truth, not opinion, and we will eat the fruit of our trustful obedience: divine life and salvation from the

Lord. The fruit is readily available in the form of the Catechism and Church teachings from the pope and bishops. It is essential to make constant use of it in order to grow strong in the faith.

PRAYER

O God, you have never abandoned your people. Even after we have sinned, you reveal yourself and give us the means to know and love you, and walk on the road to salvation. You have spoken through the Law and the Prophets in times past, and now you have given us the gift of Magisterial teaching to guide us in the way of truth. Grant us, also, the gift of docility so that we may hear and obey your every word rather than trusting in our own desires. Let us flee the praise of men and seek always your approval so that we may live in the hope of attaining heaven. Amen.

GOSPEL

Jesus moved about within Galilee; he did not wish to travel in Judea, because the Jews were trying to kill him. But the Jewish feast of Tabernacles was near.

But when his brothers had gone up to the feast, he himself also went up, not openly but as it were in secret.

Some of the inhabitants of Jerusalem said, "Is he not the one they are trying to kill? And look, he is speaking openly and they say nothing to him. Could the authorities have realized that he is the Christ? But we know where he is from. When the Christ comes, no one will know where he is from." So Jesus cried out in the temple area as he was teaching and said, "You know me and also know where I am from. Yet I did not come on my own, but the one who sent me, whom you do not know, is true. I know him, because I am from him, and he sent me." So they tried to arrest him, but no one laid a hand upon him, because his hour had not yet come.

JOHN 7: 1-2, 10, 25-30

ST. THOMAS AQUINAS

[John] presents their evil intention when he says, "They therefore wanted to seize him." Because our Lord said to them, "whom you do not know," they became angry, feigning that they did know him. And so they formed the evil plan of seizing him, so that they could crucify and kill him: "Go after him, and seize him" (Ps 70:11). Yet there are some who have Christ within themselves, and still seek to seize him in a reverent manner: "I will go up to the palm tree and seize its fruit" (Song 7:8). And so the Apostle says "I will go after it to seize it" (Phil 3:12). (Comm. John, ch. 7, 3.1067)

REFLECTION

The Pharisees were angry because the teachings of Christ had cut them to the quick. Their own stubbornness prevented them from converting to his message, indeed, to him. They claimed to know God. Christ is God and preaches nothing but godliness. If godliness were in the hearts of the Pharisees, they would have sought Jesus, not to kill him, but to know him and his true origin. Their hearts would have been open to Jesus so that he could enter in and reign in their lives.

St. Thomas says that there are some who have Christ in themselves. He plays on the word "seize." Whereas the Pharisees wanted to seize Jesus, that is, to arrest him in order to do away with him, those who are Christ's followers in our day also want to seize him, but "in a reverent manner." They want to take hold of Jesus in every way possible. Thus, St. Thomas refers to the verse in the Song of Songs. The verse actually applies to the bridegroom who desires to take hold of his bride (we can think of Christ and the Church), but the inverse is also true, as when we desire to take hold of Christ.

How do we seize Christ? First, we take hold of him when we pray, that is, when we close out the noise and distractions of the world and enter into that secret chamber of our hearts and bring him there. In the privacy of our soul, we speak intimately with him in praise, thanksgiving and adoration, and we listen to his voice speaking the secrets of his heart to us. We must seek him daily. Second, we take hold of Christ when we receive him in Holy Communion. What a wonderful taking hold of the Lord this is! He humbles himself to be taken by us completely, Body and Blood, Soul and Divinity. As the Fathers of the Church have taught, this food is not made part of our bodies; rather we are transformed into him. In Holy Communion, we want to make the most of the opportunity to speak to Christ from the depths of our heart, allowing ourselves to be lost in him at this supreme moment of the day. Thirdly, we seize Christ when we serve the poor, whether those in material poverty or spiritual poverty. In taking hold of these brothers and sisters, broken in body or soul, to care for them, we are also holding Christ in them and ministering to him through them.

Let us always remember, of course, that it he who has first seized us and who takes us into himself.

PRAYER

Lord Jesus, who humbled yourself even to the point of being pursued by those who wanted to arrest you and end your life, and who, indeed, gave up your life for me, grant me the grace of pursuing you in holiness of life. Make me cling to you always and in every moment of my life; help me to find you in my own moments of darkness and inspire me to seek your face in those whose lives are broken. Amen.

GOSPEL

Some in the crowd who heard these words of Jesus said, "This is truly the Prophet." Others said, "This is the Christ." But others said, "The Christ will not come from Galilee, will he? Does not Scripture say that the Christ will be of David's family and come from Bethlehem, the village where David lived?" So a division occurred in the crowd because of him. Some of them even wanted to arrest him, but no one laid hands on him.

So the guards went to the chief priests and Pharisees, who asked them, "Why did you not bring him?" The guards answered, "Never before has anyone spoken like this man." So the Pharisees answered them, "Have you also been deceived? Have any of the authorities or the Pharisees believed in him? But this crowd, which does not know the law, is accursed." Nicodemus, one of their members who had come to him earlier, said to them, "Does our law condemn a man before it first hears him and finds out what he is doing?" They answered and said to him, "You are not from Galilee also, are you? Look and see that no prophet arises from Galilee."

Then each went to his own house.

JOHN 7: 40-53

ST. THOMAS AQUINAS

Nicodemus said what he did because he believed in Christ and wanted to convert them to Christ; yet because he was afraid, he did not act very candidly. He thought that if they would only listen to Christ, the words of Christ would be so effective that perhaps they would be changed like those whom they sent to Jesus, and who, when they heard Christ, were turned aside from the very act for which they had been sent. (Comm. John, ch. 7, 5.1115)

REFLECTION

The temple guards, whom the Pharisees had sent to arrest Jesus, returned empty-handed but with minds and hearts that had come into contact with the truth of Christ's teaching. It was more than just words that had affected them, for they testify that it was the way that Jesus spoke that prevented them from accomplishing their deed. Indeed, it was the person of the Word, the second Person of the Trinity, whom they had met.

The same thing happened to Nicodemus who came to Jesus at night for fear of being seen with him in broad daylight. As St. Thomas says, he believed in Jesus but was afraid, and so covered his tracks.

The other leaders, to the contrary, closed their minds and hearts to Christ. They had their law and wanted to live by it alone. They were blind to the Lawgiver in their midst, who could teach them the law of love and so fulfill the law to the *nth* degree, minus, of course, the hundreds of back-breaking customs which had become encrusted onto the law of God as so many barnacles on a ship's hull.

It is not enough, though, to listen to Christ and walk away, as did the guards who reported to the chief priests and Pharisees. At some later time, when the pressures of life and cares of the world beset us, one will easily forget the experience of divine grace and he will return to his unconverted ways. Nor is it enough to listen to Christ only under cover of darkness, or to be timid in living one's faith in him, as in the case of Nicodemus. One modern-day approach of such so-called

Christianity is to claim to personally adhere to our Lord's teaching but to say that it is not necessarily good, or essential, for others. This is a relativizing of the truth.

We who have received the power of the Holy Spirit to begin our conversion (for the catechumen) or to live as followers of Christ (for the baptized) have the very same grace as the apostles to live fearlessly in the light, proclaiming the truth of who is Christ. Even in the midst of opposition we take shelter in him, as the Psalmist bids us in the responsorial psalm at today's liturgy of the word: "O Lord, my God, in you I take refuge." We can be trusting lambs following the Lamb of God, for our hope and our glory is in him alone. Nothing else, and no one else, can save us. That's the absolute truth!

PRAYER,

O God of light and truth, grant me the grace of living in the freedom of the children of God; may all that I say and do be always motivated by deep humility and great love of you. May I never shrink from doing what is right or hide my faith, so that, following you, I may attain to everlasting joy and peace with you in heaven. Amen.

FIFTH WEEK
OF
LENT

GOSPEL

Now a man was ill, Lazarus from Bethany, the village of Mary and her sister Martha. Mary was the one who had anointed the Lord with perfumed oil and dried his feet with her hair; it was her brother Lazarus who was ill. So the sisters sent word to Jesus saying, "Master, the one you love is ill." When Jesus heard this he said, "This illness is not to end in death, but is for the glory of God, that the Son of God may be glorified through it." Now Jesus loved Martha and her sister and Lazarus. So when he heard that he was ill, he remained for two days in the place where he was. Then after this he said to his disciples, "Let us go back to Judea." The disciples said to him, "Rabbi, the Jews were just trying to stone you, and you want to go back there?" Jesus answered, "Are there not twelve hours in a day? If one walks during the day, he does not stumble, because he sees the light of this world. But if one walks at night, he stumbles, because the light is not in him." He said this, and then told them, "Our friend Lazarus is asleep, but I am going to awaken him." So the disciples said to him, "Master, if he is asleep, he will be saved." But Jesus was talking about his death, while they thought that he meant ordinary sleep. So then Jesus said to them clearly, "Lazarus has died. And I am glad for you that I was not there, that you may believe. Let us go to him." So Thomas, called Didymus, said to his fellow disciples, "Let us also go to die with him."

When Jesus arrived, he found that Lazarus had already been in the tomb for four days. Now Bethany was near Jerusalem, only about two miles away. And many of the Jews had come to Martha and Mary to comfort them about their brother. When Martha heard that Jesus was coming, she went to meet him; but Mary sat at home. Martha said to Jesus, "Lord, if you had been here, my brother would not have died. But even now I know that whatever you ask of God, God will give you." Jesus said to her, "Your brother will rise." Martha said to him, "I know he will rise, in the resurrection on the last day." Jesus told her, "I am the resurrection and the life; whoever believes in me, even if he dies, will live, and everyone who lives and believes in me will never die. Do you believe this?" She said to him, "Yes, Lord. I have come to believe that you are the Christ, the Son of God, the one who is coming into the world."

When she had said this, she went and called her sister Mary secretly, saying, "The teacher is here and is asking for you." As soon as she heard this, she rose quickly and went to him. For Jesus had not yet come into the village, but was still where Martha had met him. So when the Jews who were with her in the house comforting her saw Mary get up quickly and go out, they followed her, presuming that she was going to the tomb to weep there. When Mary came to where Jesus was and saw him, she fell at his feet and said to him, "Lord, if you had been here, my brother would not have died." When Jesus saw her weeping and the Jews who had come with her weeping, he became perturbed and deeply troubled, and said, "Where have you laid him?" They said to him, "Sir, come and see." And Jesus wept. So the Jews said, "See how he loved him." But some of them said, "Could not the one who opened the eyes of the blind man have done something so that this man would not have died?"

So Jesus, perturbed again, came to the tomb. It was a cave, and a stone lay across it. Jesus said, "Take away the stone." Martha, the dead man's sister, said to him, "Lord, by now there will be a stench; he has been dead for four days." Jesus said to her, "Did I not tell you that if you believe you will see the glory of God?" So they took away the stone. And Jesus raised his eyes and said, "Father, I thank you for hearing me. I know that you always hear me; but because of the crowd here I have said this, that they may believe that you sent me." And when he had said this, he cried out in a loud voice, "Lazarus, come out!" The dead man came out, tied hand and foot with burial bands, and his face was wrapped in a cloth. So Jesus said to them, "Untie him and let him go."

Now many of the Jews who had come to Mary and seen what he had done began to believe in him.

JOHN 11: 1-45

Shorter form: JOHN 11:3-7, 17, 20-27, 33b-45
Longer form may be optionally read on any day in the fifth week of Lent

ST. THOMAS AQUINAS

*Augustine . . . says that Martha answers, ["I believe that you are the Christ, the Son of the living God"], because it gives the reason for all that our Lord had said. It is as though she were saying: Whatever you say about your power and the effect of salvation, I believe it all; because I believe something more, which is the root of all these things, that is, "that you are the Christ, the Son of the living God." Martha's profession is complete, for she professes Christ's dignity, his nature and his mission. (*Comm. John*, ch. 11, 4.1519–20)*

REFLECTION

Christ's dignity, St. Thomas explains, is as king and priest, for he is the anointed one, as his name, Christ, reveals. He was anointed with the invisible oil of the Holy Spirit. His "nature is divine and equal to the Father," for he is the Son of the living God. His mission is signified by her words, "who is coming into the world," meaning that he assumed human flesh.

In this encounter with Martha and Mary upon the death of their brother and Jesus' friend, Lazarus, our Lord explains why he came into the world. The raising of Lazarus from the dead is the sign that what Jesus does for Lazarus after four days in the tomb he will do for all who believe in him, with this difference: the final resurrection is eternal. The resurrection of the body and eternal life with God are central to Christianity on account of who God is. Having created the world and especially man as his beloved creature made in his own image, God does not find it within himself to abandon us. Thus, the Son has come into the world for us. He empties himself for us. He suffers and dies and rises from the dead for us. The "for us" means that he brings us to participate in his life, so that we might experience the resurrection.

"I believe it all," Aquinas interprets from the words of Martha, in response to Jesus' explanation that her brother would rise again. This is a line worth a lifetime of contemplation: "I believe it all." It's not a matter of picking and choosing which parts of Christ's teaching we like and then try to follow them. Nor is it a matter of choosing even most of his doctrine. No one can properly call himself a Christian who only follows Christ part way, any more than someone can set off to visit Rome but be satisfied to make it to New York. Faith requires the complete surrender of ourselves to the will of God. But the will of God is always perfect for our needs, always good, the proof of which is found in the raising of Lazarus and the effort Christ expends in order to give us a share in eternal life. One wonders, then, why there could be any hesitancy to join Martha and allow Christ's power to have full reign in our lives. We trade our short time on earth for eternity, our ever-devaluating possessions for divine glory. God wants us to be alive forever with him, to rise from the dead. Do we?

PRAYER

God all-powerful, who created the heavens and the earth for the happiness of mankind, you sent your Son to re-create what our sins have broken and destroyed in order to grant us the even greater dignity of living with you forever in eternal beatitude. Grant us the grace each day of assenting to you and your every plan for our good, so that professing our faith in you, we may, with St. Martha, truly believe it all. Amen.

GOSPEL

Some Greeks who had come to worship at the Passover Feast came to Philip, who was from Bethsaida in Galilee, and asked him, "Sir, we would like to see Jesus." Philip went and told Andrew; then Andrew and Philip went and told Jesus. Jesus answered them, "The hour has come for the Son of Man to be glorified. Amen, amen, I say to you, unless a grain of wheat falls to the ground and dies, it remains just a grain of wheat; but if it dies, it produces much fruit. Whoever loves his life loses it, and whoever hates his life in this world will preserve it for eternal life. Whoever serves me must follow me, and where I am, there also will my servant be. The Father will honor whoever serves me.

"I am troubled now. Yet what should I say? 'Father, save me from this hour'? But it was for this purpose that I came to this hour. Father, glorify your name." Then a voice came from heaven, "I have glorified it and will glorify it again." The crowd there heard it and said it was thunder; but others said, "An angel has spoken to him." Jesus answered and said, "This voice did not come for my sake but for yours. Now is the time of judgement on this world; now the ruler of this world will be driven out. And when I am lifted up from the earth, I will draw everyone to myself." He said this indicating the kind of death he would die.

JOHN 12: 20-33

ST. THOMAS AQUINAS

[Just] as Christ was sent into the world as a seed that was to bear fruit, so whatever temporal goods are given to us in this life by God are not given to us as a fruit, but rather that by their means we may obtain the fruit of an eternal reward. Indeed, our very life is a temporal gift from God to us. Therefore, anyone who exposes it for Christ bears much fruit. Such a one, therefore, hates his own life, that is, he exposes his own life, and sows, for the sake of Christ, to gain life everlasting: "He that goes forth weeping, bearing seed for sowing, shall come home with shouts of joy, bringing his sheaves with him" (Ps 126:6). And the same is true of those who risk their wealth and other goods for the sake of Christ, and share them with others, to obtain life everlasting: "He who sows bountifully will also reap bountifully" (2 Cor 9:6). (Comm. John, ch. 12, 4.1645)

REFLECTION

Never has anyone taken so much as a penny beyond this world into the next life. Never has there been any human person to escape death. (Even Christ did not escape death, though by his own choice.) Why, then, do so many people, rich and poor alike, hoard wealth and possessions as if their lives depended totally on them, or as if such things would accompany these people into the next life?

Almsgiving, not to be limited to Lent even if it is more emphasized during this season, helps us to have a proper perspective on material goods. Almsgiving involves charity, and charity covers a multitude of sins (1 Peter 4:8). In other words, charity, looking for the good of another, is the true reparation for the evils we have committed. When we are intent upon building up another person's good, we are contributing to something much greater than any particular good deed; our acts of charity are transformed by God into participations in his re-creation of the world. At the same time, we grow in virtue, the only "thing" we take with us past the grave.

St. Thomas hits on the essence of the problem with material (temporal) gifts. We may confuse them as the fruit given to us that belongs to us, as if the purpose of life is to amass wealth and possessions. One way or another, we rationalize that we have earned whatever it is that we own. To whatever extent we have earned anything, since we belong to God who created us, it is all still his. Nothing is ever truly ours in terms of complete ownership, a point brought home by the fact that naked we entered the world and naked we leave (Job 1:21). Our temporal goods are, in fact, seeds to be planted, that is, used for the good of self and neighbor. Even more is this the case with our very lives. The real fruit that we reap when we sow the seeds of our gifts and our lives is eternal life. The way to have eternal life is to plant the seed of our lives in Christ. It begins in baptism and confirmation and is nourished by the Holy Eucharist and daily prayer.

PRAYER

Lord God, you have created me and formed me in your image and redeemed my life through the passion, death, and resurrection of Jesus Christ, your Son. Grant that I may be generous with my life and the goods you have given me as a steward, treating them all as so much seed to be sown, so that one day I may rejoice to be gathered in by you into your kingdom in eternal joy. Amen.

GOSPEL

Jesus went to the Mount of Olives. But early in the morning he arrived again in the temple area, and all the people started coming to him, and he sat down and taught them. Then the scribes and the Pharisees brought a woman who had been caught in adultery and made her stand in the middle. They said to him, "Teacher, this woman was caught in the very act of committing adultery. Now in the law, Moses commanded us to stone such women. So what do you say?" They said this to test him, so that they could have some charge to bring against him. Jesus bent down and began to write on the ground with his finger. But when they continued asking him, he straightened up and said to them, "Let the one among you who is without sin be the first to throw a stone at her." Again he bent down and wrote on the ground. And in response, they went away one by one, beginning with the elders. So he was left alone with the woman before him. Then Jesus straightened up and said to her, "Woman, where are they? Has no one condemned you?" She replied, "No one, sir." Then Jesus said, "Neither do I condemn you. Go, and from now on do not sin any more."

JOHN 8: 1-11

ST. THOMAS AQUINAS

Jesus cautions [the woman] when he says, "Go, and do not sin again."
There were two things in that woman: her nature and her sin. Our Lord
could have condemned both. For example, he could have condemned her
nature if he had ordered them to stone her, and he could have condemned
her sin if he had not forgiven her. He was also able to absolve each. For
example, if he had given her license to sin, saying: "Go, live as you wish,
and put your hope in my freeing you. No matter how much you sin, I will
free you even from Gehenna and from the tortures of hell." But our Lord
does not love sin, and does not favor wrongdoing, and so condemned her
sin but not her nature, saying, "Go, and do not sin again." We see here
how kind our Lord is because of his gentleness, and how just he is because
of his truth. (Comm. John, ch. 8, 1.1139)

REFLECTION

St. Thomas notes that neither justice nor mercy is served by ignor-
ing the reality of sin or wrongdoing. The relativistic refusal to identify
sin as such makes both justice and mercy superfluous. It is as if one
might treat cancer as a hang nail in the hope of avoiding the requisite
surgery to save one's life. Such is often the case in our day when referring to weaknesses of the flesh. We do the opposite of the Pharisees;
we pretend that sin is okay, the norm, since "everybody's doing it."

St. Thomas's distinction amounts to this: that God hates the sin
but loves the sinner. It's an important difference provided that sin is
recognized for what it is. The distinction is difficult, if not impossible;
to apply if sin is redefined simply as part of human nature, that being
human means to err, even morally. The trouble with this way of thinking is that human nature is identified as something corrupt. Those
Christians who maintain this mindset think that grace is merely the
covering over of our shame so that God does not have to see it. The
truth of the matter is that we are not utterly corrupt and that being
human, truly and fully human, means that we are created to flourish.
Grace is not an external but an interior reality and gift by which we

are transformed so that we can attain to full human happiness in the eternal vision of God.

Presumption is the sin of thinking that our sins are not offensive to God, as St. Thomas explains above. Condemnation of human nature, on the other hand, is the sin of thinking that we ourselves are repugnant to God. Both extremes are false. The actuality is that we all do things contrary to our true happiness, and this is offensive to God because he made us to be happy and flourish in his company. What is needed is repentance, standing before Christ just as we are in broad daylight. Only this humble position allows Christ to heal the wounds of our sins with his true judgment and mercy, drawing us more deeply into his divine friendship.

PRAYER

Lord Jesus Christ, I want to know you and the power flowing from your resurrection. Grant me the grace of continual conversion of heart, so that, by uniting my penances with your suffering, I may arrive at resurrection from the dead and enjoy life with you eternally. Amen.

GOSPEL

Jesus went to the Mount of Olives. But early in the morning he arrived again in the temple area, and all the people started coming to him, and he sat down and taught them. Then the scribes and the Pharisees brought a woman who had been caught in adultery and made her stand in the middle. They said to him, "Teacher, this woman was caught in the very act of committing adultery. Now in the law, Moses commanded us to stone such women. So what do you say?" They said this to test him, so that they could have some charge to bring against him. Jesus bent down and began to write on the ground with his finger. But when they continued asking him, he straightened up and said to them, "Let the one among you who is without sin be the first to throw a stone at her." Again he bent down and wrote on the ground. And in response, they went away one by one, beginning with the elders. So he was left alone with the woman before him. Then Jesus straightened up and said to her, "Woman, where are they? Has no one condemned you?" She replied, "No one, sir." Then Jesus said, "Neither do I condemn you. Go, and from now on do not sin any more."

JOHN 8: 1-11

ST. THOMAS AQUINAS

Here the question arises as to whether a sinful judge sins by passing sentence against another person who has committed the same sin. . . . My answer to this is that two distinctions have to be made. For the judge is either continuing in his determination to sin, or he has repented of his sins; and again, he is either punishing as a minister of the law or on his own initiative. Now if he has repented of his sin, he is no longer a sinner, and so he can pass sentence without sinning. But if he continues in his determination to sin, he does not sin in passing sentence if he does this as a minister of the law; although he would be sinning by doing the very things for which he deserves a similar sentence. But if he passes sentence on his own authority, then I say that he sins in passing sentence, because he is not doing this out of a love for justice, but from some evil root; otherwise he would first punish in himself what he notices in someone else, because "A just person is the first to accuse himself" (Prov 18:17). (Comm. John, ch. 8, 1.1133)

REFLECTION

While it is not the Christian's business to pass judgment on the interior life of another person (which is distinct from passing judgment on the goodness or evilness of exterior actions), Divine Revelation tells us that "all have sinned and fall short of the glory of God" (Rom 3:23 RSV). We may safely make the judgment that we are all, save for the Blessed Virgin Mary, sinners. Yet, Christians also bear the responsibility to be the "salt of the earth" and the "light of the world" (Matt 5:13–16); we must help others to know and love Jesus Christ and his Church. This presumes a growing familiarity with our Lord's teachings, both from the Scriptures and his speaking through the successors of his apostles, the bishops. In this sense, then, each Christian is appointed to know the truths of Christianity, both doctrinal and moral, and to teach them to others. There is no room for passivity in this regard, only docility to the Holy Spirit.

One of the fruits of our Lenten conversion and resolve is a deeper desire for knowledge of the truth of our Catholic faith. Reading the Catechism and other good Catholic literature, participating in parish lectures and discussions, parish missions, and listening more attentively to the prayers at Mass as well as the homilies all help us to have the kind of knowledge necessary for us to share the faith with others. Both our actions and our conversations reveal to others what we believe; more importantly, we want others to share in the friendship we have experienced with Christ.

It is a lie that our own past sinfulness makes us unworthy witnesses for Christ and the Church. As St. Thomas points out, if we have repented of our sins, then we are no longer sinners in the sense of being outside of communion with God. Even if we continue to struggle with the same weakness or sins, so long as we are repenting and making frequent use of the sacrament of penance, we have our role and responsibility to share the best news about man, that salvation is possible for all.

Another lie that sometimes creeps in is the false judgment that all religions are equal. If this were true, there would be less reason to be Christian, for Catholicism makes demands on us that other religions do not. But, more to the point, Christianity is a religion revealed by God. If it were merely human, it wouldn't matter. However, since God is its author, we cannot err in following him. Any other claim that a religion makes to be revealed must have its claims measured against this most divine revelation. Since truth is one, a discovery of something contrary to Christianity shows itself to have failed the judgment we are each capable of making. Our religion is not something we make up as we go along. God has given it to us. When we stand on this truth, guided by the valid successors of the Apostles, we can be confident of never judging religious realities incorrectly.

PRAYER

Lord, make us heralds of your gospel of truth. Enlighten our minds and fire our hearts with the grace of the Holy Spirit; give us holy and prudent bishops and priests to guide us so that we may see and judge all things rightly and always act according to your holy will. Amen.

In Year C, when the preceding Gospel is read on Sunday, the following text is used.

GOSPEL

Jesus spoke to them again, saying, "I am the light of the world. Whoever follows me will not walk in darkness, but will have the light of life." So the Pharisees said to him, "You testify on your own behalf, so your testimony cannot be verified." Jesus answered and said to them, "Even if I do testify on my own behalf, my testimony can be verified, because I know where I came from and where I am going. But you do not know where I come from or where I am going. You judge by appearances, but I do not judge anyone. And even if I should judge, my judgment is valid, because I am not alone, but it is I and the Father who sent me. Even in your law it is written that the testimony of two men can be verified. I testify on my behalf and so does the Father who sent me." So they said to him, "Where is your father?" Jesus answered, "You know neither me nor my Father. If you knew me, you would know my Father also." He spoke these words while teaching in the treasury in the temple area. But no one arrested him, because his hour had not yet come.

JOHN 8: 12-20

ST. THOMAS AQUINAS

The effect of this light is to expel darkness; and so he says, "Whoever follows me will not walk in darkness." Because this light is universal, it universally expels all darkness. Now there are three kinds of darkness. There is the darkness of ignorance: "They have neither known nor understood; they walk in darkness" (Ps 81:5); and this is the darkness reason has of itself, insofar as it is darkened of itself. There is the darkness of sin: "You were at one time darkness, but now you are light in the Lord" (Eph 5:8). This darkness belongs to human reason not of itself, but from the affections which, by being badly disposed by passion or habit, seek something as good that is not really good. Further, there is the darkness of eternal damnation: "Cast the unprofitable servant into the exterior darkness" (Mt 25:30). The first two kinds of darkness are found in this life; but the third is at the end of life. Thus, "Whoever follows me will not walk in darkness": the darkness of ignorance, because I am the truth; nor the darkness of sin, because I am the way; nor the darkness of eternal damnation, because I am the life.

He next adds the fruit of his teaching, "but he will have the light of life," for one who has the light is outside the darkness of damnation. He says, "Whoever follows me," because just as one who does not want to stumble in the dark has to follow the one who is carrying the light, so one who wants to be saved must, by believing and loving, follow Christ, who is the light. This is the way the apostles followed him (Matt 4). Because physical light can fail because it sets, it happens that one who follows it meets with darkness. But the light we are talking about here does not set and never fails; consequently, one who follows it has an unfailing light, that is, an unfailing light of life. For the light that is visible does not give life, but gives us an external aid because we live insofar as we have understanding, and this is a certain participation in this light. And when this light completely shines upon us we will then have perfect life: "With you is the fountain of life, and in your light we will see the light" (Ps 35:10). This is the same as saying: We will have perfectly or completely when we see this light as it is. Thus we read further on: "This is eternal life: that they know you, the only true God and Jesus Christ, whom you have sent" *(John 17:3). (Comm. John,* ch. 8, 2.1144–45)

REFLECTION

The Old Testament story of Susanna, wrongly accused of adultery by two old lecherous judges because she refused to give in to their advances, shows how much the human heart is able to retreat into darkness, closing itself off from the light (see Daniel 13). In the context of the account of the woman caught in adultery in the Gospel of John, our Lord reveals himself as the light of the world. The leading men of the city were ready to stone her when Christ passes judgment on them instead: Let the one without sin be the first to cast a stone. They all slinked away. Such is the true yet merciful judgment of deeds seen in his light.

Oh, to possess such light within ourselves! And yet we do, beginning from the moment we are baptized. The sacrament of penance removes anything that shadows his light in us. Every reception of the Holy Eucharist is an opportunity to allow that light to intensify in our souls. Thus may we become ablaze with the glory of the Lord.

PRAYER

O Christ, my light and my joy, set me aflame with love of you; burn away every impurity in me; let your glory illuminate my mind; make my heart ardent for you alone; may your brilliance suffuse every part of my being; till I am but one with you. Amen.

GOSPEL

JESUS SAID TO THE PHARISEES:

"I am going away and you will look for me, but you will die in your sin. Where I am going you cannot come." So the Jews said, "He is not going to kill himself, is he, because he said, 'Where I am going you cannot come'?" He said to them, "You belong to what is below, I belong to what is above. You belong to this world, but I do not belong to this world. That is why I told you that you will die in your sins. For if you do not believe that I AM, you will die in your sins." So they said to him, "Who are you?" Jesus said to them, "What I told you from the beginning. I have much to say about you in condemnation. But the one who sent me is true, and what I heard from him I tell the world." They did not realize that he was speaking to them of the Father. So Jesus said to them, "When you lift up the Son of Man, then you will realize that I AM, and that I do nothing on my own, but I say only what the Father taught me. The one who sent me is with me. He has not left me alone, because I always do what is pleasing to him." Because he spoke this way, many came to believe in him.

JOHN 8: 21-30

ST. THOMAS AQUINAS

[Jesus] says . . . that they ought to come to the faith by means of his passion: "So Jesus said to them: When you have lifted up the Son of Man, then you will understand." He is saying in effect: You do not know now that God is my Father, but "when you have lifted up the Son of Man," that is, when you have nailed me to the wood of the cross, "then you will understand," that is, some of you will understand by faith. "And I, if I am lifted up from the earth, will draw all things to myself" (John 12:32). And so, as Augustine says, he recalls the sufferings of his cross to give hope to sinners, so that no one will despair, no matter what his crime, or think that he is too evil, since the very people who crucified Christ are freed from their sins by Christ's blood. For there is no sinner so great that he cannot be freed by the blood of Christ. (Comm. John, ch. 8, 3.1191)

REFLECTION

Whereas the serpent that Moses mounted on a pole so that whoever looked at it might be healed was only a temporary remedy (see Num 21: 4–9), Christ's lifting up on the cross gives eternal life for all who come to him, that is, who approach the power of his cross given us through the sacraments of the Church. Hence, the Christian rejoices to say: "O death, where is your victory? O death, where is your sting?" (1 Cor 15:55).

The sacramental life enables the Christian to continually participate in the power of Christ's cross. The divine grace of each sacrament corresponds in an analogous way to natural life. Baptism is our rebirth in Christ. Confirmation makes us adult witnesses for Christ. The Holy Eucharist is our divine food. Marriage is for the building up of the family in Christ. Holy Orders makes a man an instrument of the grace necessary for eternal life and gives order to the life of the Church. Penance heals us of the effects of sins committed after baptism, and anointing of the sick heals the effects of sin and prepares us, at the end of life, for our journey to heaven. Every one of our ills and difficulties in this life can be submitted to the power of the cross through the sacraments.

St. Thomas remarks on Augustine's insight that our Lord wants no one to despair of his healing power, no matter how bad we may think things are. Only the devil decries us with discouraging denunciations. Jesus desires that we always remember that his forgiveness reaches everyone, even those who put him on the cross.

As a reminder of that love, look often upon the crucifix. Keep it displayed in a prominent place to remind you of the greatest love and mercy that the world will ever know. Call upon the powerful and healing blood of Christ.

PRAYER

Lord Jesus Christ, you desired to be lifted up on the cross so that we could be healed of all our sins and miseries. Be merciful to me, a sinner. Draw me into deeper contemplation of your wounds, and open arms, as I gaze upon the Crucifix. Infuse into my soul deep sentiments of trust in your divine mercy and your power to heal me of all my sins. Amen.

GOSPEL

Jesus said to those Jews who believed in him, "If you remain in my word, you will truly be my disciples, and you will know the truth, and the truth will set you free." They answered him, "We are descendants of Abraham and have never been enslaved to anyone. How can you say, 'You will become free'?" Jesus answered them, "Amen, amen, I say to you, everyone who commits sin is a slave of sin. A slave does not remain in a household forever, but a son always remains. So if the Son frees you, then you will truly be free. I know that you are descendants of Abraham. But you are trying to kill me, because my word has no room among you. I tell you what I have seen in the Father's presence; then do what you have heard from the Father."

They answered and said to him, "Our father is Abraham." Jesus said to them, "If you were Abraham's children, you would be doing the works of Abraham. But now you are trying to kill me, a man who has told you the truth that I heard from God; Abraham did not do this. You are doing the works of your father!" So they said to him, "We were not born of fornication. We have one Father, God." Jesus said to them, "If God were your Father, you would love me, for I came from God and am here; I did not come on my own, but he sent me."

JOHN 8: 31-42

175

ST. THOMAS AQUINAS

Yet the greatest thing is the acquisition of freedom, which the knowledge of the truth produces in those who believe. Thus he says, "and the truth will make you free." In this context, to free does not mean a release from some confinement, as the Latin language suggests, but rather a being made free; and this is from three things. The truth of this doctrine will free us from the error of falsity: "My mouth will speak the truth; my lips will hate wickedness" (Prov 8:7). The truth of grace will free us from the slavery to sin: "The law of the Spirit of life in Christ Jesus has freed me from the law of sin and of death" (Rom 8:2). And the truth of eternity, in Christ Jesus, will free us from corruption: "The creature will be freed from its slavery to corruption" (Rom 8:21). (Comm. John, ch. 8, 4.1199)

REFLECTION

The first reading at Mass today (Dan. 3: 14-20, 91-92, 95) is the account of the three young men in the furnace who refused to worship a false idol. They were thrown into a blazing furnace fettered, when the king looked in he saw them walking about freely. It was not only that they miraculously survived the conflagration that converted the king, but also their walking in freedom broke the shackles binding his heart.

Jesus tells us in the gospel that the truth will make us free. St. Thomas highlights the difference between freedom as a release from confinement and freedom that gives full reign to the human intellect and will. For many a saint and martyr has maintained the second even at the expense of the first. The examples abound, but we might consider St. Thomas More, the good friend and confidant of King Henry VIII, who refused to barter the truth about Henry's usurpation of power over the Church and suffered imprisonment and beheading as a reward. Yet he had been made free: from the error of falsity, from sin, and eternal and interior death. Thomas knew the truth: that Henry was only a man, while the true head of the Church was the successor of the poor fisherman chosen by Christ. Thomas knew that Henry might be a king, but he could never remit one sin or change one host into the body of Christ. Thomas lived freely in the truth. Henry died imprisoned in his guilt.

Freedom properly understood is not the ability to avoid the confines or strictures of following rules; it is, rather, the opportunity to achieve human excellence. In other words, freedom is the gift that God gives us to say yes to the offer of divine life and eternal happiness. He does not want us to say "no," but he will not force us to say yes. More confounding than some of the greatest Christian mysteries is why anyone would refuse such a gift. In the end, the apparent escape from the so-called confinement (from rules) leads to a greater slavery to some lesser good. What pain it must be to wake up one day to find that for this meager sum one has sold one's soul to the devil's blandishments and deceits for a lie.

The ultimate example of freedom is found in Christ laying down his life for us, nailed to the cross. Even death could not confine him, as we know from his resurrection. Nor can death confine us because we have divine life of the Blessed Trinity in our souls. We have died with him in baptism and now live his resurrected life. We await the Day of Judgment with joy, knowing that we shall be like him in glory. In the meantime, we are free because we belong to Christ, the Truth.

PRAYER

You, Lord God, have given me freedom to live and thrive in your creation and in your truth. Help me with your grace, that my steps may be guided by you and that your light may shine upon my path until I reach my heavenly homeland to live with you forever. Amen.

GOSPEL

JESUS SAID TO THE JEWS:

"Amen, amen, I say to you, whoever keeps my word will never see death." So the Jews said to him, "Now we are sure that you are possessed. Abraham died, as did the prophets, yet you say, 'Whoever keeps my word will never taste death.' Are you greater than our father Abraham, who died? Or the prophets, who died? Who do you make yourself out to be?" Jesus answered, "If I glorify myself, my glory is worth nothing; but it is my Father who glorifies me, of whom you say, 'He is our God.' You do not know him, but I know him. And if I should say that I do not know him, I would be like you a liar. But I do know him and I keep his word. Abraham your father rejoiced to see my day; he saw it and was glad." So the Jews said to him, "You are not yet fifty years old and you have seen Abraham?" Jesus said to them, "Amen, amen, I say to you, before Abraham came to be, I AM." So they picked up stones to throw at him; but Jesus hid and went out of the temple area.

JOHN 8: 51-59

ST. THOMAS AQUINAS

Then when he says, "your father Abraham rejoiced that he was to see my day," he gives his answer to the first question asked by the Jews: "Are you greater than our father Abraham?" He shows that he is greater for the following reason: Whoever waits for someone as for his good and perfection is less than the one he waits for; but Abraham placed the entire hope of his perfection and good in me; therefore, he is less than I. In regard to this he says, your father Abraham, in whom you glory, "rejoiced that he was to see my day; he saw it and was glad." (Comm. John, ch. 8, 8.1287)

REFLECTION

In the gospel passage Jesus teaches that whoever keeps Christ's word, which is truth, will never *see* death. He is referring to spiritual and eternal death (the experience of the damned in hell). The Pharisees twist his words, claiming that our Lord said that such a one would never *taste* death. For them, to see and taste meant the same thing because they were thinking only in terms of physical death. If we belong to Christ, even if we taste physical death (and we must), we will not see eternal death. Moreover, we have the sure promise of the resurrection of our bodies, so that even the taste of death is at most a passing encounter.

Interestingly, it is the religious authorities who bring up Abraham, negatively comparing Jesus to him. Our Lord uses this as the opportunity to show that Abraham lived by faith and awaited and expected Christ, the Messiah. Yet, when the Messiah, whom the Jews also await, stands in their presence, they fail to recognize him. They do not believe what he is telling them about himself. They fail to believe that God would come to them in the person of Jesus Christ, even after witnessing his miracles. They reject Jesus' testimony and replace it with their own distorted thinking, reaching the conclusion that they must kill Jesus.

If it were merely a matter of some difficulty in grasping the profundity of Jesus' revelation, we might sympathize with the Pharisees and their ilk. The reality, however, is that they did not really know God although they claimed to be on intimate terms with him. They had hardened their hearts and closed their ears to any possibility of God's word reaching into their souls. We might say that they refused to so much as even taste Life. Such was their disobedience and the root of their hatred of Jesus. Thus, when Jesus tells them that he is greater than Abraham and that Abraham rejoiced to see his day, rather than rejoicing with Abraham's joy, they can only reach for rocks to throw.

Christ lives. For this reason we need never fear death, nor any other difficulty or suffering in our lives. He is greater than all, more powerful than any evil, and those who put their trust in his word, will see his glory in heaven with Abraham and all the holy ones who have trusted God rather than themselves.

PRAYER

O Lord, your word is life and truth, and I trust in you alone. Let me never be duped by distorted thoughts or lies, or the clever words of mere men. Keep me fixed on your truth and grant that I may come, one day, to see you face to face. Amen.

GOSPEL

The Jews picked up rocks to stone Jesus. Jesus answered them, "I have shown you many good works from my Father. For which of these are you trying to stone me?" The Jews answered him, "We are not stoning you for a good work but for blasphemy. You, a man, are making yourself God." Jesus answered them, "Is it not written in your law, 'I said, "You are gods"'? If it calls them gods to whom the word of God came, and Scripture cannot be set aside, can you say that the one whom the Father has consecrated and sent into the world blasphemes because I said, 'I am the Son of God'? If I do not perform my Father's works, do not believe me; but if I perform them, even if you do not believe me, believe the works, so that you may realize and understand that the Father is in me and I am in the Father." Then they tried again to arrest him; but he escaped from their power.

He went back across the Jordan to the place where John first baptized, and there he remained. Many came to him and said, "John performed no sign, but everything John said about this man was true." And many there began to believe in him.

JOHN 10: 31-42

ST. THOMAS AQUINAS

The Evangelist says, "The Jews took up stones again to stone him."
They were hard of heart and unable to understand his profound message;
and so, being like stones, they resort to stones: "When I spoke to them they
fought against me without cause" (Ps 199:7).

The Evangelist shows their inflexibility by the fact that after so many
confirmations of the truth, after the evidence of so many miracles and
wonders, they still persist in their evil. So "again they tried to arrest him,"
to apprehend him, not in order to believe and understand, but in their
rage to do him harm; they were even the more enraged because he had
more clearly expressed his equality with the Father: "They hold fast to
deceit, they refuse to return" (Jer 8:5). (Comm. John, ch. 10, 6.1453,
1468)

REFLECTION

Once again Jesus eludes the grasp of his adversaries. It will not be
long before he is finally arrested. St. Thomas reminds us that it is not
by luck that the authorities are able to pluck Jesus off the street. He is
God and is in control. He chooses the time and place for being taken.
He gives his life freely. Even his arguments with the learned religious
men are calculated to give them the opportunity to see the truth of his
words that he is God's Son and that he performs his Father's works.
They remain, however, stonyhearted and pick up stones to throw at
Jesus, as St. Thomas says.

To be a follower of Christ is to have a mind and heart converted
to the truth of the gospel. There is no middle ground for a Christian,
no possibility of living in both camps. Soon enough, the follower of
Christ is as mystified by the hard-hearted ways of the world as we are
continually bewildered by the inability of the Jewish leaders to see the
simple truth in Christ's words and deeds. We are struck by the perverse twists by which sin is considered good, and the good is thought
to be absurd. For example, simply reflect on the issue of abortion. Not
a small number of people think of abortion as a good thing, giving a

false freedom to women to choose to terminate the life of an unborn person. Or, to use a stronger example, we might discuss infanticide, the killing of a newly born baby. Millions of innocent babies are killed annually, and this action is protected under cover of law, while those who speak in defense of life are often vilified.

As Christ's disciples we will encounter, in one situation or another, souls who resist the truth of Christianity, and even the more basic truth of the moral life, that is, natural law (the human or rational participation in the way God made things to be). Our best plan of action, if we are to be instruments in the divine hand, is to grow in love for God and to rely on his strength alone. We can only do this by staying close to Jesus in prayer and meeting him in the sacraments, most especially the Eucharist, and studying the truths of our faith. Our love for God will necessarily translate into love for persons when we interact with those who need the gospel, because real love always goes outside to others. Nothing less will work. Love alone will enable us to suffer a little with Christ and for him.

PRAYER

Lord, you alone are my love, my refuge and my strength. You shelter my soul and fill me with your Spirit. Make me your witness to all those you send into my life; hear my prayer for all those who this day have no one to pray for their conversion. Amen.

GOSPEL

Many of the Jews who had come to Mary and seen what Jesus had done began to believe in him. But some of them went to the Pharisees and told them what Jesus had done. So the chief priests and the Pharisees convened the Sanhedrin and said, "What are we going to do? This man is performing many signs. If we leave him alone, all will believe in him, and the Romans will come and take away both our land and our nation." But one of them, Caiaphas, who was high priest that year, said to them, "You know nothing, nor do you consider that it is better for you that one man should die instead of the people, so that the whole nation may not perish." He did not say this on his own, but since he was high priest for that year, he prophesied that Jesus was going to die for the nation, and not only for the nation, but also to gather into one the dispersed children of God. So from that day on they planned to kill him.

So Jesus no longer walked about in public among the Jews, but he left for the region near the desert, to a town called Ephraim, and there he remained with his disciples.

Now the Passover of the Jews was near, and many went up from the country to Jerusalem before Passover to purify themselves. They looked for Jesus and said to one another as they were in the temple area, "What do you think? That he will not come to the feast?"

JOHN 11: 45-56

ST. THOMAS AQUINAS

It was the miracles of Christ that raised their problem; so they said, "What are we to do? For this man performs many signs." They were blind, for they still called him a man after such a great demonstration of his divinity. As he himself said: "The works which the Father has granted me to accomplish, these very works which I am doing, bear me witness" (John 5:35). In truth, they were no less foolish than the blind because they wondered what they should do, whereas there was nothing for them to do but believe: "What signs do you do, that we may see, and believe you?" (John 6:30). See how many signs he did work! Even they said, "this man performs many signs:" "Their wickedness blinded them" (Wis 2:21). (Comm. John, ch. 11, 7.1569)

REFLECTION

The gospel passage for today follows the account of the raising of Lazarus from the dead by Jesus, an event that stirred many to belief while causing others to harden their hearts against Jesus. St. Thomas notes the paradox of the situation when he points out that the Pharisees and chief priests admitted that Jesus worked many signs, yet even these were not enough for them to see that he was no ordinary man, to see his divine work.

In yet another ironic twist, Caiaphas, the high priest, counseled that Jesus should be put to death rather than lose the entire nation. His counsel was prophetic, for Christ took sin and death upon himself so that all people of all times might become the nation of God, the people of God, and be saved from perishing.

What crime did the Sanhedrin see in the miracles of Jesus? No crime at all. Rather, they feared losing their influence over the people: "If we leave him alone, all will believe in him." They wanted the people to revere them, to obey them alone. One might wonder if they even truly cared that their people should love and obey God. Rather than concern for the salvation of the people as well as their own, "they backed away from salvation and took others with themselves" (*Comm.*

John, ch. 11, 7.1570).

If only all people were to believe in Jesus and follow him, how much different our cities, our nations, our world would be! If only our hearts were completely subject to the kingship of Christ. How different we would be by allowing his grace to transform us, by allowing Christ complete lordship in every aspect of our lives!

PRAYER

Lord Jesus Christ, Son of the living God, have mercy on me, a sinner. Make me your own and guard me as one of your flock. Send the pervasive power of your grace to convert my heart completely to you and your divine will for my good and my salvation, and that of my land. Make me a sign of your love to all the world. Amen.

HOLY
WEEK

GOSPEL

AT THE PROCESSION WITH PALMS

When Jesus and the disciples drew near Jerusalem and came to Bethphage on the Mount of Olives, Jesus sent two disciples, saying to them, "Go into the village opposite you, and immediately you will find an ass tethered, and a colt with her. Untie them and bring them here to me. And if anyone should say anything to you, reply, 'The master has need of them.' Then he will send them at once." This happened so that what had been spoken through the prophet might be fulfilled: / *Say to daughter Zion, / "Behold, your king comes to you, / meek and riding on an ass, / and on a colt, the foal of a beast of burden." /* The disciples went and did as Jesus had ordered them. They brought the ass and the colt and laid their cloaks over them, and he sat upon them. The very large crowd spread their cloaks on the road, while others cut branches from the trees and strewed them on the road. The crowds preceding him and those following kept crying out and saying: / "Hosanna to the Son of David; / blessed is the he who comes in the name of the Lord; / hosanna in the highest." / And when he entered Jerusalem the whole city was shaken and asked, "Who is this?" And the crowds replied, "This is Jesus the prophet, from Nazareth in Galilee."

MATTHEW 21: 1-11

GOSPEL

MASS

One of the Twelve, who was called Judas Iscariot, went to the chief priests and said, "What are you willing to give me if I hand him over to you?" They paid him thirty pieces of silver, and from that time on he looked for an opportunity to hand him over.

On the first day of the Feast of Unleavened Bread, the disciples approached Jesus and said, "Where do you want us to prepare for you to eat the Passover?" He said, "Go into the city to a certain man and tell him, 'The teacher says, "My appointed time draws near; in your house I shall celebrate the Passover with my disciples."'" The disciples then did as Jesus had ordered, and prepared the Passover.

When it was evening, he reclined at table with the Twelve. And while they were eating, he said, "Amen, I say to you, one of you will betray me." Deeply distressed at this, they began to say to him one after another, "Surely it is not I, Lord?" He said in reply, "He who has dipped his hand into the dish with me is the one who will betray me. The Son of Man indeed goes, as it is written of him, but woe to that man by whom the Son of Man is betrayed. It would be better for that man if he had never been born." Then Judas, his betrayer, said in reply, "Surely it is not I, Rabbi?" He answered, "You have said so."

While they were eating, Jesus took bread, said the blessing, broke it, and giving it to his disciples said, "Take and eat; this is my body." Then he took a cup, gave thanks, and gave it to them, saying, "Drink from it, all of you, for this is my blood of the covenant, which will be shed on behalf of many for the forgiveness of sins. I tell you, from now on I shall not drink this fruit of the vine until the day when I drink it with you new in the kingdom of my Father." Then, after singing a hymn, they went out to the Mount of Olives.

Then Jesus said to them, "This night all of you will have your faith in me shaken, for it is written: / *I will strike the shepherd,* / *and the sheep of the flock will be dispersed;* / but after I have been raised up, I shall go before you to Galilee." Peter said to him in reply, "Though all may have their faith in you shaken, mine will never be." Jesus said to him, "Amen, I say to you, this very night before the cock crows, you will deny me three times." Peter said to him, "Even though I should have to die with you, I will not deny you." And all the disciples spoke likewise.

Then Jesus came with them to a place called Gethsemane, and he said to his disciples, "Sit here while I go over there and pray." He took along Peter and the two sons of Zebedee, and began to feel sorrow and distress. Then he said to them, "My soul is sorrowful even to death. Remain here and keep watch with me." He advanced a little and fell prostrate in prayer, saying, "My Father, if it is possible, let this cup pass from me; yet, not as I will, but as you will." When he returned to his disciples he found them asleep. He said to Peter, "So you could not keep watch with me for one hour? Watch and pray that you may not undergo the test. The spirit is willing, but the flesh is weak." Withdrawing a second time, he prayed again, "My Father, if it is not possible that this cup pass without my drinking it, your will be done!" Then he returned once more and found them asleep, for they could not keep their eyes open. He left them and withdrew again and prayed a third time, saying the same thing again. Then he returned to his disciples and said to them, "Are you still sleeping and taking your rest? Behold, the hour is at hand when the Son of Man is to be handed over to sinners. Get up, let us go. Look, my betrayer is at hand."

While he was still speaking, Judas, one of the Twelve, arrived, accompanied by a large crowd, with swords and clubs, who had come from the chief priests and the elders of the people. His betrayer had arranged a sign with them, saying, "The man I shall kiss is the one; arrest him." Immediately he went over to Jesus and said, "Hail, Rabbi!" and he kissed him. Jesus answered him, "Friend, do what you have come for." Then stepping forward they laid hands on Jesus and arrested him. And behold, one of those who accompanied Jesus put his hand to his sword, drew it, and struck the high priest's servant, cutting off his ear. Then Jesus said to him, "Put your sword back into its sheath, for all who take the sword will perish by the sword. Do you think that I cannot call upon my Father and he will not provide me at this moment with more than twelve legions of angels? But then how would the Scriptures be fulfilled which say that it must come to pass in this way?" At that hour Jesus said to the crowds, "Have you come out as against a robber, with swords and clubs to seize me? Day after day I sat teaching in the temple area, yet you did not arrest me. But all this has come to pass that the writings of the prophets may be fulfilled." Then all the disciples left him and fled.

Those who had arrested Jesus led him away to Caiaphas the high priest, where the scribes and the elders were assembled. Peter was following him at a distance as far as the high priest's courtyard, and going inside he sat down with the servants to see the outcome. The chief priests and the entire Sanhedrin kept trying to obtain false testimony against Jesus in order to put him to death, but they found none, though many false witnesses came forward. Finally two came forward who stated, "This man said, 'I can destroy the temple of God and within three days rebuild it.'" The high priest rose and addressed him, "Have you no answer? What are these men testifying against you?" But Jesus was silent. Then the high priest said to him, "I order you to tell us under oath before the living God whether you are the Christ, the Son of God." Jesus said to him in reply, "You have said so. But I tell you: / From now on you will see 'the Son of Man / seated at the right hand of the Power' / and 'coming on the clouds of heaven.'" / Then the high priest tore his robes and said, "He has blasphemed! What further need have we of witnesses? You have now heard the blasphemy; what is your opinion?" They said in reply, "He deserves to die!" Then they spat in his face and struck him, while some slapped him, saying, "Prophesy for us, Christ: who is it that struck you?"

Now Peter was sitting outside in the courtyard. One of the maids came over to him and said, "You too were with Jesus the Galilean." But he denied it in front of everyone, saying, "I do not know what you are talking about!" As he went out to the gate, another girl saw him and said to those who were there, "This man was with Jesus the Nazorean." Again he denied it with an oath, "I do not know the man!" A little later the bystanders came over and said to Peter, "Surely you too are one of them; even your speech gives you away." At that he began to curse and to swear, "I do not know the man." And immediately a cock crowed. Then Peter remembered the word that Jesus had spoken: "Before the cock crows you will deny me three times." He went out and began to weep bitterly.

When it was morning, all the chief priests and the elders of the people took counsel against Jesus to put him to death. They bound him, led him away, and handed him over to Pilate, the governor.

Then Judas, his betrayer, seeing that Jesus had been condemned, deeply regretted what he had done. He returned the thirty pieces of silver to the chief priests and elders, saying, "I have sinned in betraying innocent blood." They said, "What is that to us? Look to it yourself." Flinging the money into the temple, he departed and went off and hanged himself. The chief priests gathered up the money, but said, "It is not lawful to deposit this in the temple treasury, for it is the price of blood." After consultation, they used it to buy the potter's field as a burial place for foreigners. That is why that field even today is called the Field of Blood. Then was fulfilled what had been said through Jeremiah the prophet, / *And they took the thirty pieces of silver,* / *the value of a man with a price on his head,* / *a price set by some of the Israelites,* / *and they paid it out for the potter's field* / *just as the Lord had commanded me.*

Now Jesus stood before the governor, who questioned him, "Are you the king of the Jews?" Jesus said, "You say so." And when he was accused by the chief priests and elders, he made no answer. Then Pilate said to him, "Do you not hear how many things they are testifying against you?" But he did not answer him one word, so that the governor was greatly amazed.

Now on the occasion of the feast the governor was accustomed to release to the crowd one prisoner whom they wished. And at that time they had a notorious prisoner called Barabbas. So when they had assembled, Pilate said to them, "Which one do you want me to release to you, Barabbas, or Jesus called Christ?" For he knew that it was out of envy that they had handed him over. While he was still seated on the bench, his wife sent him a message, "Have nothing to do with that righteous man. I suffered much in a dream today because of him." The chief priests and the elders persuaded the crowds to ask for Barabbas but to destroy Jesus. The governor said to them in reply, "Which of the two do you want me to release to you?" They answered, "Barabbas!" Pilate said to them, "Then what shall I do with Jesus called Christ?" They all said, "Let him be crucified!" But he said, "Why? What evil has he done?" They only shouted the louder, "Let him be crucified!" When Pilate saw that he was not succeeding at all, but that a riot was breaking out instead, he took water and washed his hands in the sight of the crowd, saying, "I am innocent of this man's blood. Look to it yourselves." And the whole people said in reply, "His blood be upon us and upon our children." Then he released Barabbas to them, but after he had Jesus scourged, he handed him over to be crucified.

Then the soldiers of the governor took Jesus inside the praetorium and gathered the whole cohort around him. They stripped off his clothes and threw a scarlet military cloak about him. Weaving a crown out of thorns, they placed it on his head, and a reed in his right hand. And kneeling before him, they mocked him, saying, "Hail, King of the Jews!" They spat upon him and took the reed and kept striking him on the head. And when they had mocked him, they stripped him of the cloak, dressed him in his own clothes, and led him off to crucify him.

As they were going out, they met a Cyrenian named Simon; this man they pressed into service to carry his cross.

And when they came to a place called Golgotha — which means Place of the Skull —, they gave Jesus wine to drink mixed with gall. But when he had tasted it, he refused to drink. After they had crucified him, they divided his garments by casting lots; then they sat down and kept watch over him there. And they placed over his head the written charge against him: This is Jesus, the King of the Jews. Two revolutionaries were crucified with him, one on his right and the other on his left. Those passing by reviled him, shaking their heads and saying, "You who would destroy the temple and rebuild it in three days, save yourself, if you are the Son of God, and come down from the cross!" Likewise the chief priests with the scribes and elders mocked him and said, "He saved others; he cannot save himself. So he is the king of Israel! Let him come down from the cross now, and we will believe in him. He trusted in God; let him deliver him now if he wants him. For he said, 'I am the Son of God.'" The revolutionaries who were crucified with him also kept abusing him in the same way.

From noon onward, darkness came over the whole land until three in the afternoon. And about three o'clock Jesus cried out in a loud voice, *"Eli, Eli, lema sabachthani?"* which means, "My God, my God, why have you forsaken me?" Some of the bystanders who heard it said, "This one is calling for Elijah." Immediately one of them ran to get a sponge; he soaked it in wine, and putting it on a reed, gave it to him to drink. But the rest said, "Wait, let us see if Elijah comes to save him." But Jesus cried out again in a loud voice, and gave up his spirit.

Here all kneel and pause for a short time.

And behold, the veil of the sanctuary was torn in two from top to bottom. The earth quaked, rocks were split, tombs were opened, and the bodies of many saints who had fallen asleep were raised. And coming forth from their tombs after his resurrection, they entered the holy city and appeared to many. The centurion and the men with him who were keeping watch over Jesus feared greatly when they saw the earthquake and all that was happening, and they said, "Truly, this was the Son of God!" There were many women there, looking on from a distance, who had followed Jesus from Galilee, ministering to him. Among them were Mary Magdalene and Mary the mother of James and Joseph, and the mother of the sons of Zebedee.

When it was evening, there came a rich man from Arimathea named Joseph, who was himself a disciple of Jesus. He went to Pilate and asked for the body of Jesus; then Pilate ordered it to be handed over. Taking the body, Joseph wrapped it in clean linen and laid it in his new tomb that he had hewn in the rock. Then he rolled a huge stone across the entrance to the tomb and departed. But Mary Magdalene and the other Mary remained sitting there, facing the tomb.

The next day, the one following the day of preparation, the chief priests and the Pharisees gathered before Pilate and said, "Sir, we remember that this impostor while still alive said, 'After three days I will be raised up.' Give orders, then, that the grave be secured until the third day, lest his disciples come and steal him and say to the people, 'He has been raised from the dead.' This last imposture would be worse than the first." Pilate said to them, "The guard is yours; go, secure it as best you can." So they went and secured the tomb by fixing a seal to the stone and setting the guard.

MATTHEW 26: 14-75 & 27: 1-66

Shorter form: MATTHEW 27:11-54

ST. THOMAS AQUINAS

[The Evangelist] mentions how [the people] conducted themselves. And first of all, what they did: "they took branches of palm trees." Now the palm, since it retains its freshness, signifies victory. Thus in antiquity it was conferred upon conquerors as a symbol of their victory. Again, we read in Revelation (7:9) of the conquering martyrs that they held "palm branches in their hands." And so the branches of palm trees were given as praise, signifying victory, because our Lord was to conquer death by dying and to triumph over Satan, the prince of death, by the victory of the cross. "And went out to meet him:" "Prepare to meet your God, O Israel!" (Amos 4:12).

Secondly, the Evangelist mentions what they said: they shouted out

Hosanna! Blessed is he who comes in the name of the Lord, the King of Israel! Here they combine both petition and praise. There is petition when they say, Hosanna, that is "Save us, I implore you." It is like saying: "hosy," which means "save," and "anna," which means "implore." According to Augustine, this is not a word, but rather an exclamation of one praying. And it is quite proper that they should ask the Lord Jesus for salvation, because we read in Isaiah (35:4): "Behold your God . . . He will come and save you;" "Stir up thy might, and come to save us!" (Ps 80:2). (Comm. John, ch. 12, 3.1620–21)

REFLECTION

Only several days after this triumphal entry into Jerusalem, the people will be talked into turning against Jesus. Cries of "crucify him" will replace today's "Hosannas." We rightfully shudder at the prospect of having to join that murderous crowd's frenzied cries for the blood of Jesus to be poured out, and much prefer to acclaim him with our hosannas. Yet we can find a spiritual relationship between the two expressions. "Hosanna," St. Thomas explains, means "save us, we pray." The way that God chose to save us is the crucifixion of Jesus, his death on the cross, and his resurrection from the dead. Thus, we cry out for salvation as we pray the Sanctus (Holy, Holy, Holy . . .) at Mass, just before that sacred moment when we hear Christ's words on the lips of the priest, "This is my Body . . . this is my Blood . . . ," given and poured out for the remission of sins. The Church teaches us that our prayer for salvation is answered in the sacrifice of the Cross, renewed on the altar in the Holy Eucharist, the Body and Blood, Soul and Divinity of Jesus Christ made sacramentally present.

Let us, indeed, shudder to think of having to say those words: "Crucify him." Let us, rather, prepare our hearts to receive him, as did the people with their cloaks and olive branches. Receive him in Holy Communion as your king who enters your soul humbly under the simple external signs of bread and wine. Beg him that his crucifixion and death and resurrection would continue to transform every moment of life: that past sins be healed, that the present moment be a continual awareness of his nearness, and that the promise of future glory may be fulfilled.

PRAYER

Praise to you, O most holy Lord of salvation. May you stir up your might and come to save us through your suffering and death. Make us victorious over sin, and help us to prepare our hearts to receive you as our king. Bring us to the peace of the heavenly Jerusalem where we will enjoy your company forever. Amen.

GOSPEL

PROCESSION WITH PALMS

When Jesus and his disciples drew near to Jerusalem, to Bethpage and Bethany at the Mount of Olives, he sent two of his disciples and said to them, "Go into the village opposite you, and immediately on entering it, you will find a colt tethered on which no one has ever sat. Untie it and bring it here. If anyone should say to you, 'Why are you doing this?' reply, 'The Master has need of it and will send it back here at once.'" So they went off and found a colt tethered at a gate outside on the street, and they untied it. Some of the bystanders said to them, "What are you doing, untying the colt?" They answered them just as Jesus had told them to, and they permitted them to do it. So they brought the colt to Jesus and put their cloaks over it. And he sat on it. Many people spread their cloaks on the road, and others spread leafy branches that they had cut from the fields. Those preceding him as well as those following kept crying out: / "Hosanna! / Blessed is he who comes in the name of the Lord! / Blessed is the kingdom of our father David that is to come! / Hosanna in the highest!"

MARK 11: 1-10

Alternative: JOHN 12:12-16

GOSPEL

MASS

The Passover and the Feast of Unleavened Bread were to take place in two days' time. So the chief priests and the scribes were seeking a way to arrest him by treachery and put him to death. They said, "Not during the festival, for fear that there may be a riot among the people."

When he was in Bethany reclining at table in the house of Simon the leper, a woman came with an alabaster jar of perfumed oil, costly genuine spikenard. She broke the alabaster jar and poured it on his head. There were some who were indignant. "Why has there been this waste of perfumed oil? It could have been sold for more than three hundred days' wages and the money given to the poor." They were infuriated with her. Jesus said, "Let her alone. Why do you make trouble for her? She has done a good thing for me. The poor you will always have with you, and whenever you wish you can do good to them, but you will not always have me. She has done what she could. She has anticipated anointing my body for burial. Amen, I say to you, wherever the gospel is proclaimed to the whole world, what she has done will be told in memory of her."

Then Judas Iscariot, one of the Twelve, went off to the chief priests to hand him over to them. When they heard him they were pleased and promised to pay him money. Then he looked for an opportunity to hand him over.

On the first day of the Feast of Unleavened Bread, when they sacrificed the Passover lamb, his disciples said to him, "Where do you want us to go and prepare for you to eat the Passover?" He sent two of his disciples and said to them, "Go into a city and a man will meet you, carrying a jar of water. Follow him. Wherever he enters, say to the master of the house, 'The Teacher says, "Where is my guest room where I may eat the Passover with my disciples?"' Then he will show you a large upper room furnished and ready. Make the preparations for us there."

The disciples then went off, entered the city, and found it just as he had told them; and they prepared the Passover.

When it was evening, he came with the Twelve. And as they reclined at table and were eating, Jesus said, "Amen, I say to you, one of you will betray me, one who is eating with me." They began to be distressed and to say to him, one by one, "Surely it is not I?" He said to them, "One of the Twelve, the one who dips with me into the dish. For the Son of Man indeed goes, as it is written of him, but woe to that man by whom the Son of Man is betrayed. It would be better for that man if he had never been born."

While they were eating, he took bread, said the blessing, broke it, and gave it to them, and said, "Take it; this is my body." Then he took a cup, gave thanks, and gave it to them, and they all drank from it. He said to them, "This is my blood of the covenant, which will be shed for many. Amen, I say to you, I shall not drink again the fruit of the vine until the day when I drink it new in the kingdom of God." Then, after singing a hymn, they went out to the Mount of Olives.

Then Jesus said to them, "All of you will have your faith shaken, for it is written: / *I will strike the shepherd,* / *and the sheep will be dispersed.* / But after I have been raised up, I shall go before you to Galilee." Peter said to him, "Even though all should have their faith shaken, mine will not be." Then Jesus said to him, "Amen, I say to you, this very night before the cock crows twice you will deny me three times." But he vehemently replied, "Even though I should have to die with you, I will not deny you." And they all spoke similarly.

Then they came to a place named Gethsemane, and he said to his disciples, "Sit here while I pray." He took with him Peter, James and John, and began to be troubled and distressed. Then he said to them, "My soul is sorrowful even to death. Remain here and keep watch." He advanced a little and fell to the ground and prayed that if it were possible the hour might pass by him; he said, "Abba, Father, all things are possible to you. Take this cup away from me, but not what I will but what you will." When he returned he found them asleep. He said to

Peter, "Simon, are you asleep? Could you not keep watch for one hour? Watch and pray that you may not undergo the test. The spirit is willing but the flesh is weak." Withdrawing again, he prayed, saying the same thing. Then he returned once more and found them asleep, for they could not keep their eyes open and did not know what to answer him. He returned a third time and said to them, "Are you still sleeping and taking your rest? It is enough. The hour has come. Behold, the Son of Man is to be handed over to sinners. Get up, let us go. See, my betrayer is at hand."

Then, while he was still speaking, Judas, one of the Twelve, arrived, accompanied by a crowd with swords and clubs who had come from the chief priests, the scribes, and the elders. His betrayer had arranged a signal with them, saying, "The man I shall kiss is the one; arrest him and lead him away securely." He came and immediately went over to him and said, "Rabbi." And he kissed him. At this they laid hands on him and arrested him. One of the bystanders drew his sword, struck the high priest's servant, and cut off his ear. Jesus said to them in reply, "Have you come out as against a robber, with swords and clubs, to seize me? Day after day I was with you teaching in the temple area, yet you did not arrest me; but that the Scriptures may be fulfilled." And they all left him and fled. Now a young man followed him wearing nothing but a linen cloth about his body. They seized him, but he left the cloth behind and ran off naked.

They led Jesus away to the high priest, and all the chief priests and the elders and the scribes came together. Peter followed him at a distance into the high priest's courtyard and was seated with the guards, warming himself at the fire. The chief priests and the entire Sanhedrin kept trying to obtain testimony against Jesus in order to put him to death, but they found none. Many gave false witness against him, but their testimony did not agree. Some took the stand and testified falsely against him, alleging, "We heard him say, 'I will destroy this temple made with hands and within three days I will build another not made with hands.'" Even so their testimony did not agree. The high priest rose before the assembly and questioned Jesus, saying, "Have you no answer? What are these men testifying against you?" But he was silent and answered nothing. Again the high priest asked him and said to him, "Are you the Christ, the son of the Blessed One?" Then Jesus answered, "I am; / and you will see the Son of Man / seated at the right hand of the Power / and coming with the clouds of heaven." / At that the high priest tore his garments and said, "What further need have we of witnesses? You have heard the blasphemy. What do you think?" They all condemned him as deserving to die. Some began to spit on him. They blindfolded him and struck him and said to him, "Prophesy!" And the guards greeted him with blows.

While Peter was below in the courtyard, one of the high priest's maids came along. Seeing Peter warming himself, she looked intently at him and said, "You too were with the Nazarene, Jesus." But he denied it saying, "I neither know nor understand what you are talking about." So he went out into the outer court. Then the cock crowed. The maid saw him and began again to say to the bystanders, "This man is one of them." Once again he denied it. A little later the bystanders said to Peter once more, "Surely you are one of them; for you too are a Galilean." He began to curse and to swear, "I do not know this man about whom you are talking." And immediately a cock crowed a second time. Then Peter remembered the word that Jesus had said to him, "Before the cock crows twice you will deny me three times." He broke down and wept.

As soon as morning came, the chief priests with the elders and the scribes, that is, the whole Sanhedrin held a council. They bound Jesus, led him away, and handed him over to Pilate. Pilate questioned him, "Are you the king of the Jews?" He said to him in reply, "You say so." The chief priests accused him of many things. Again Pilate questioned him, "Have you no answer? See how many things they accuse you of." Jesus gave him no further answer, so that Pilate was amazed.

Now on the occasion of the feast he used to release to them one prisoner whom they requested. A man called Barabbas was then in prison along with the rebels who had committed murder in a rebellion. The crowd came forward and began to ask him to do for them as he was accustomed. Pilate answered, "Do you want me to release to you the king of the Jews?" For he knew that it was out of envy that the chief priests had handed him over. But the chief priests stirred up the crowd to have him release Barabbas for them instead. Pilate again said to them in reply, "Then what do you want me to do with the man you call the king of the Jews?" They shouted again, "Crucify him." Pilate said to them, "Why? What evil has he done?" They only shouted the louder, "Crucify him." So Pilate, wishing to satisfy the crowd, released Barabbas to them and, after he had Jesus scourged, handed him over to be crucified.

The soldiers led him away inside the palace, that is, the praetorium, and assembled the whole cohort. They clothed him in purple and, weaving a crown of thorns, placed it on him. They began to salute him with, "Hail, King of the Jews!" and kept striking his head with a reed and spitting upon him. They knelt before him in homage. And when they had mocked him, they stripped him of the purple cloak, dressed him in his own clothes, and led him out to crucify him.

They pressed into service a passer-by, Simon, a Cyrenian, who was coming in from the country, the father of Alexander and Rufus, to carry his cross.

They brought him to the place of Golgotha—which is translated Place of the Skull—. They gave him wine drugged with myrrh, but he did not take it. Then they crucified him and divided his garments by casting lots for them to see what each should take. It was nine o'clock in the morning when they crucified him. The inscription of the charge against him read, "The King of the Jews." With him they crucified two revolutionaries, one on his right and one on his left. Those passing by reviled him, shaking their heads and saying, "Aha! You who would destroy the temple and rebuild it in three days, save yourself by coming down from the cross." Likewise the chief priests, with the scribes, mocked him among themselves and said, "He saved others; he cannot save himself. Let the Christ, the King of Israel, come down now from the cross that we may see and believe." Those who were crucified with him also kept abusing him. At noon darkness came over the whole land until three in the afternoon. And at three o'clock Jesus cried out in a loud voice, *"Eloi, Eloi, lema sabachthani?"* which is translated, "My God, my God, why have you forsaken me?" Some of the bystanders who heard it said, "Look, he is calling Elijah." One of them ran, soaked a sponge with wine, put it on a reed and gave it to him to drink saying, "Wait, let us see if Elijah comes to take him down." Jesus gave a loud cry and breathed his last.

Here all kneel and pause for a short time.

The veil of the sanctuary was torn in two from top to bottom. When the centurion who stood facing him saw how he breathed his last he said, "Truly this man was the Son of God!" There were also women looking on from a distance. Among them were Mary Magdalene, Mary the mother of the younger James and of Joses, and Salome. These women had followed him when he was in Galilee and ministered to him. There were also many other women who had come up with him to Jerusalem.

When it was already evening, since it was the day of preparation, the day before the sabbath, Joseph of Arimathea, a distinguished member of the council, who was himself awaiting the kingdom of God, came and courageously went to Pilate and asked for the body of Jesus. Pilate was amazed that he was already dead. He summoned the centurion and asked him if Jesus had already died. And when he learned of it from the centurion, he gave the body to Joseph. Having bought a linen cloth, he took him down, wrapped him in the linen cloth, and laid him in a tomb that had been hewn out of the rock. Then he rolled a stone against the entrance to the tomb. Mary Magdalene and Mary the mother of Joses watched where he was laid.

MARK 14: 1-72 & 15: 1-47

Shorter form: MARK 15:1-39

ST. THOMAS AQUINAS

They praise [Jesus] for two things: for his coming and for the power of his reign or kingdom. They praise his coming when they say, "Blessed is he who comes in the name of the Lord." Note that to bless is to speak good things. Now God blesses us in one way, and we bless God in another way. For when God blesses us he makes us good, since for God to speak is to do: "For he commanded [that is, spoke], and they were created" (Ps 148:5). But when we bless God, we profess his goodness: "We bless you from the house of the Lord" (Ps 118:26); "Blessed be every one who blesses you!" (Gen 27:29). Therefore, "Blessed is he who comes in the name of the Lord," for Christ worked in the name of God, because every thing he did he directed to the glory of God. (Comm. John, ch. 12, 3.1622)

REFLECTION

God is continually blessing us. He is continually holding us in being. Our goodness derives from the fact that God loves us. In addition to holding us in his creating hand, God constantly sends us gifts of grace that affect us, both spiritually and materially. Sometimes people fall into the trap of thinking that God is not thinking of them, or that God is not blessing them. Nothing could be further from the truth. Only the devil would suggest such an evil lie to us, on account of his own hatred of God and man. In fact, we often fail to notice the blessings that are given to us, or account them as too small. When this happens, we become like a friend for whom nothing is good enough from the one who seeks to show us love. We become ungrateful and complaining. The antidote is to spend time daily meditating on the thousands of blessings God sends us and has given us, not the least of which is our very existence. The path to holiness entails a spirit of gratitude and praise with each step we take, supported as we are by God at our side. No sin can prevent God from loving us and drawing us back to himself with countless blessings.

Moreover, when we acknowledge the limitless graces and blessings we have received from God, we fulfill our duty to worship him. We are blessing him by professing his goodness, as St. Thomas explains. Indeed, we might even say that the one thing that we can give God that he does not have is our gratitude and praise. He does not force his sons and daughters to love him; he waits for us to freely give ourselves to him. While he possesses us as his creatures, he who is love never violates our free will. Thus, we make a gift of our lives to him, offered anew each day and throughout each day.

Christ desires to enter more deeply into our lives so that we can experience what it means to be truly and fully human, to bring us to fulfillment in him. His plan is only for blessing for each one of us. May we invite him to be the king of love reigning in our hearts; let us adore him with heartfelt praise.

PRAYER

Heavenly Father, it is right and just to give you praise always and everywhere for the many gifts and graces you have given us, especially through the passion, death and resurrection of Jesus Christ, our Lord. Increase in us a spirit of thanksgiving and praise, particularly through the worth reception of the Most Holy Eucharist, the Body and Blood of your Son. Amen.

GOSPEL

PROCESSION WITH PALMS

Jesus proceeded on his journey up to Jerusalem. As he drew near to Bethpage and Bethany at the place called the Mount of Olives, he sent two of his disciples. He said, "Go into the village opposite you, and as you enter it you will find a colt tethered on which no one has ever sat. Untie it and bring it here. And if anyone should ask you, 'Why are you untying it?' you will answer, 'The Master has need of it.'" So those who had been sent went off and found everything just as he had told them. And as they were untying the colt, its owners said to them, "Why are you untying this colt?" They answered, "The Master has need of it." So they brought it to Jesus, threw their cloaks over the colt, and helped Jesus to mount. As he rode along, the people were spreading their cloaks on the road; and now as he was approaching the slope of the Mount of Olives, the whole multitude of his disciples began to praise God aloud with joy for all the mighty deeds they had seen. They proclaimed: / "Blessed is the king who comes / in the name of the Lord. / Peace in heaven / and glory in the highest." / Some of the Pharisees in the crowd said to him, "Teacher, rebuke your disciples." He said in reply, "I tell you, if they keep silent, the stones will cry out!"

LUKE 19: 28-40

GOSPEL

MASS

When the hour came, Jesus took his place at table with the apostles. He said to them, "I have eagerly desired to eat this Passover with you before I suffer, for, I tell you, I shall not eat it again until there is fulfillment in the kingdom of God." Then he took a cup, gave thanks, and said, "Take this and share it among yourselves; for I tell you that from this time on I shall not drink of the fruit of the vine until the kingdom of God comes." Then he took the bread, said the blessing, broke it, and gave it to them, saying, "This is my body, which will be given for you; do this in memory of me." And likewise the cup after they had eaten, saying, "This cup is the new covenant in my blood, which will be shed for you.

"And yet behold, the hand of the one who is to betray me is with me on the table; for the Son of Man indeed goes as it has been determined; but woe to that man by whom he is betrayed." And they began to debate among themselves who among them would do such a deed.

Then an argument broke out among them about which of them should be regarded as the greatest. He said to them, "The kings of the Gentiles lord it over them and those in authority over them are addressed as 'Benefactors'; but among you it shall not be so. Rather, let the greatest among you be as the youngest, and the leader as the servant. For who is greater: the one seated at table or the one who serves? Is it not the one seated at table? I am among you as the one who serves. It is you who have stood by me in my trials; and I confer a kingdom on you, just as my Father has conferred one on me, that you may eat and drink at my table in my kingdom; and you will sit on thrones judging the twelve tribes of Israel.

"Simon, Simon, behold Satan has demanded to sift all of you like wheat, but I have prayed that your own faith may not fail; and once you have turned back, you must strengthen your brothers." He said to him, "Lord, I am prepared to go to prison and to die with you." But he replied, "I tell you, Peter, before the cock crows this day, you will deny three times that you know me."

He said to them, "When I sent you forth without a money bag or a sack or sandals, were you in need of anything?" "No, nothing," they replied. He said to them, "But now one who has a money bag should take it, and likewise a sack, and one who does not have a sword should sell his cloak and buy one. For I tell you that this Scripture must be fulfilled in me, namely, *He was counted among the wicked;* and indeed what is written about me is coming to fulfillment." Then they said, "Lord, look, there are two swords here." But he replied, "It is enough!"

Then going out, he went, as was his custom, to the Mount of Olives, and the disciples followed him. When he arrived at the place he said to them, "Pray that you may not undergo the test." After withdrawing about a stone's throw from them and kneeling, he prayed, saying, "Father, if you are willing, take this cup away from me; still, not my will but yours be done." And to strengthen him an angel from heaven appeared to him. He was in such agony and he prayed so fervently that his sweat became like drops of blood falling on the ground. When he rose from prayer and returned to his disciples, he found them sleeping from grief. He said to them, "Why are you sleeping? Get up and pray that you may not undergo the test."

While he was still speaking, a crowd approached and in front was one of the Twelve, a man named Judas. He went up to Jesus to kiss him. Jesus said to him, "Judas, are you betraying the Son of Man with a kiss?" His disciples realized what was about to happen, and they asked, "Lord, shall we strike with a sword?" And one of them struck the high priest's servant and cut off his right ear. But Jesus said in reply, "Stop, no more of this!" Then he touched the servant's ear and healed him. And Jesus said to the chief priests and temple guards and elders who had come for him, "Have you come out as against a robber, with swords and clubs? Day after day I was with you in the temple area, and you did not seize me; but this is your hour, the time for the power of darkness."

After arresting him they led him away and took him into the house of the high priest; Peter was following at a distance. They lit a fire in the middle of the courtyard and sat around it, and Peter sat down with them. When a maid saw him seated in the light, she looked intently at him and said, "This man too was with him." But he denied it saying, "Woman, I do not know him." A short while later someone else saw him and said, "You too are one of them"; but Peter answered, "My friend, I am not." About an hour later, still another insisted, "Assuredly, this man too was with him, for he also is a Galilean." But Peter said, "My friend, I do not know what you are talking about." Just as he was saying this, the cock crowed, and the Lord turned and looked at Peter; and Peter remembered the word of the Lord, how he had said to him, "Before the cock crows today, you will deny me three times." He went out and began to weep bitterly. The men who held Jesus in custody were ridiculing and beating him. They blindfolded him and questioned him, saying, "Prophesy! Who is it that struck you?" And they reviled him in saying many other things against him.

When day came the council of elders of the people met, both chief priests and scribes, and they brought him before their Sanhedrin. They said, "If you are the Christ, tell us," but he replied to them, "If I tell you, you will not believe, and if I question, you will not respond. But from this time on the Son of Man will be seated at the right hand of the power of God." They all asked, "Are you then the Son of God?" He replied to them, "You say that I am." Then they said, "What further need have we for testimony? We have heard it from his own mouth."

Then the whole assembly of them arose and brought him before Pilate. They brought charges against him, saying, "We found this man misleading our people; he opposes the payment of taxes to Caesar and maintains that he is the Christ, a king." Pilate asked him, "Are you the king of the Jews?" He said to him in reply, "You say so." Pilate then addressed the chief priests and the crowds, "I find this man not guilty." But they were adamant and said, "He is inciting the people with his teaching throughout all Judea, from Galilee where he began even to here."

On hearing this Pilate asked if the man was a Galilean; and upon learning that he was under Herod's jurisdiction, he sent him to Herod, who was in Jerusalem at that time. Herod was very glad to see Jesus; he had been wanting to see him for a long time, for he had heard about him and had been hoping to see him perform some sign. He questioned him at length, but he gave him no answer. The chief priests and scribes, meanwhile, stood by accusing him harshly. Herod and his soldiers treated him contemptuously and mocked him, and after clothing him in resplendent garb, he sent him back to Pilate. Herod and Pilate became friends that very day, even though they had been enemies formerly. Pilate then summoned the chief priests, the rulers, and the people and said to them, "You brought this man to me and accused him of inciting the people to revolt. I have conducted my investigation in your presence and have not found this man guilty of the charges you have brought against him, nor did Herod, for he sent him back to us. So no capital crime has been committed by him. Therefore I shall have him flogged and then release him."

But all together they shouted out, "Away with this man! Release Barabbas to us." —Now Barabbas had been imprisoned for a rebellion that had taken place in the city and for murder.— Again Pilate addressed them, still wishing to release Jesus, but they continued their shouting, "Crucify him! Crucify him!" Pilate addressed them a third time, "What evil has this man done? I found him guilty of no capital crime. Therefore I shall have him flogged and then release him." With loud shouts, however, they persisted in calling for his crucifixion, and their voices prevailed. The verdict of Pilate was that their demand should be granted. So he released the man who had been imprisoned for rebellion and murder, for whom they asked, and he handed Jesus over to them to deal with as they wished.

As they led him away they took hold of a certain Simon, a Cyrenian, who was coming in from the country; and after laying the cross on him, they made him carry it behind Jesus. A large crowd of people followed Jesus, including many women who mourned and lamented him.

Jesus turned to them and said, "Daughters of Jerusalem, do not weep for me; weep instead for yourselves and for your children for indeed, the days are coming when people will say, 'Blessed are the barren, the wombs that never bore and the breasts that never nursed.' At that time people will say to the mountains, 'Fall upon us!' and to the hills, 'Cover us!' for if these things are done when the wood is green, what will happen when it is dry?" Now two others, both criminals, were led away with him to be executed.

When they came to the place called the Skull, they crucified him and the criminals there, one on his right, the other on his left. Then Jesus said, "Father, forgive them, they know not what they do." They divided his garments by casting lots. The people stood by and watched; the rulers, meanwhile, sneered at him and said, "He saved others, let him save himself if he is the chosen one, the Christ of God." Even the soldiers jeered at him. As they approached to offer him wine they called out, "If you are King of the Jews, save yourself." Above him there was an inscription that read, "This is the King of the Jews."

Now one of the criminals hanging there reviled Jesus, saying, "Are you not the Christ? Save yourself and us." The other, however, rebuking him, said in reply, "Have you no fear of God, for you are subject to the same condemnation? And indeed, we have been condemned justly, for the sentence we received corresponds to our crimes, but this man has done nothing criminal." Then he said, "Jesus, remember me when you come into your kingdom." He replied to him, "Amen, I say to you, today you will be with me in Paradise."

It was now about noon and darkness came over the whole land until three in the afternoon because of an eclipse of the sun. Then the veil of the temple was torn down the middle. Jesus cried out in a loud voice, "Father, into your hands I commend my spirit"; and when he had said this he breathed his last.

Here all kneel and pause for a short time.

The centurion who witnessed what had happened glorified God and said, "This man was innocent beyond doubt." When all the people who had gathered for this spectacle saw what had happened, they returned home beating their breasts; but all his acquaintances stood at a distance, including the women who had followed him from Galilee and saw these events.

Now there was a virtuous and righteous man named Joseph, who, though he was a member of the council, had not consented to their plan of action. He came from the Jewish town of Arimathea and was awaiting the kingdom of God. He went to Pilate and asked for the body of Jesus. After he had taken the body down, he wrapped it in a linen cloth and laid him in a rock-hewn tomb in which no one had yet been buried. It was the day of preparation, and the sabbath was about to begin. The women who had come from Galilee with him followed behind, and when they had seen the tomb and the way in which his body was laid in it, they returned and prepared spices and perfumed oils. Then they rested on the sabbath according to the commandment.

LUKE 22: 14-71 & 23: 1-56

Shorter form: LUKE 23:1-49

ST. THOMAS AQUINAS

The king comes to you, I say, not to harm you, but to set you free; thus he adds, "sitting on an ass's colt!" This signifies the mercy of the king, which is most welcome to his subjects: "His throne is upheld by mercy" [Prov 20:28]. This is just the opposite to "A king's wrath is like the growling of a lion" (Prov 19:12). He is saying in effect: He is not coming as a haughty king—which would make him hateful—but with gentleness: "If they make you master of the feast, do not exalt yourself" (Sir 32:1). Therefore, have no fear that the king will oppress you. Now the Old Law was given in fear, because the Law produced slaves. This phrase also signifies the power of the king, because by coming with humility and in weakness he attracted the entire world: "The weakness of God is stronger than men" (1 Cor 1:25). (Comm. John, ch. 12, 3.1627)

REFLECTION

In the Passion narrative, Pilate interrogates Jesus concerning the charge brought by the chief priests that Jesus is the king of the Jews (Luke 23:3). Indeed, he is a king, for he is God, the king and maker of the universe. But he is not the type of king the religious leaders or Pilate have in mind. Jesus is the king whose reign is for the benefit of his subjects, St. Thomas tells us. Elsewhere in the gospel Christ explains that true authority is exercised on the behalf of others, to serve them, not to lord it over them, as earthly rulers do. This perhaps explains why Pilate and the others could not recognize our Lord's kingship, for they had been taught wrongly about authority.

Christ is still our king. He continues to come to us humbly, as he did on that day when he rode into Jerusalem amidst the cheering crowds who thought he had come to restore their nation. Surely he has come to restore us, just not for earthly realms. He wants us to reign with him in heaven. First, he must clarify the meaning of his kingship. So he ascends the cross, "his throne upheld by mercy," as St. Thomas puts it, and gives his life for us. Only at this last hour does our Lord allow his kingly identity to be clearly displayed for all the world to see.

We see it even in our own day wherever the crucifix is hung.

This is why Catholics want the crucifix in their churches and homes and other important places. It reminds us of the power of mercy by which we have been redeemed, Divine Mercy incarnate who, by dying, beat death at its own game. Indeed, the weakness of God is stronger than all the power of the nations.

PRAYER

Lord Jesus Christ, look upon me as I kneel before your cross. You are my king and my Lord. Grant that I may experience the healing power of your crucified love. Reign in my heart forever. Amen.

GOSPEL

Six days before Passover Jesus came to Bethany, where Lazarus was, whom Jesus had raised from the dead. They gave a dinner for him there, and Martha served, while Lazarus was one of those reclining at table with him. Mary took a liter of costly perfumed oil made from genuine aromatic nard and anointed the feet of Jesus and dried them with her hair; the house was filled with the fragrance of the oil. Then Judas the Iscariot, one of his disciples, and the one who would betray him, said, "Why was this oil not sold for three hundred days' wages and given to the poor?" He said this not because he cared about the poor but because he was a thief and held the money bag and used to steal the contributions. So Jesus said, "Leave her alone. Let her keep this for the day of my burial. You always have the poor with you, but you do not always have me."

The large crowd of the Jews found out that he was there and came, not only because of him, but also to see Lazarus, whom he had raised from the dead. And the chief priests plotted to kill Lazarus too, because many of the Jews were turning away and believing in Jesus because of him.

JOHN 12: 1-11

ST. THOMAS AQUINAS

Mystically, the pound [of nard] Mary used denotes the work of justice, for it belongs to justice to weigh things and give pound for pound: "Their weight shall be equal" [Ezek 45:11]. Now four other virtues must be added if the work of justice is to be perfect. First, compassion: and so he says, "ointment," which, because it is soothing, represents mercy: "For judgment is without mercy to one who has shown no mercy" (James 2:12). Secondly, humility is needed: so he says, "nard," which, since it is a small herb, signifies humility: "The greater you are, the more you must humble yourself" (Sir 3:18). Thirdly, faith is needed: thus he says, "pure" (pisticus), that is believing (fidelis): "The righteous shall live by his faith" (Hab 2:4). Fourthly, charity must be present: so he says, "costly," for charity alone pays the price for eternal life: "If I give away all I have . . . but have not love, I gain nothing" (1 Cor 13:3). (Comm. John, ch. 12, 1.1599)

REFLECTION

Mary knew the cost of the ointment that she seemed to be wasting on Jesus—after all, such ointments were saved for most special occasions. It came from India. Would it not have been enough if she had dabbed a bit of it on Jesus' face or head—as anointing was usually done? Instead, she pours it all out—on his feet. Extravagant! And then, to dry his feet with her hair!

Judas knew the cost of that nard, too. His complaint reveals its price: a year's worth of wages. Instead of seeing this anointing of the precious nard as a sign of love and preparation for Jesus' burial, Judas saw it as a waste. What good would this do?

Mary was pouring out more than the nard: she was pouring out her heart of love, her very self, at the feet of Jesus. It was a sign of her total self-surrender; her way of saying: Jesus, you are my only Love!

Judas could not see the purpose of this act of love, because he had closed his heart to Jesus. He could not surrender the costly nard, because he could not surrender his heart. In effect he was saying: Jesus, you are not my only love (or even, at all)! Which was to say that now Jesus was not his love at all. A few days later he would betray his Jesus, his Lord, for one-tenth of the cost of that nard! So little love.

In these last days of Lent, rather than focus on whether we have been successful in our Lenten practices, let us redirect our attention away from ourselves and to Jesus. As he surrendered himself completely for us, let us surrender our hearts to him. We are invited anew to pour out our hearts at the feet of Jesus. Is there some costly thing we have been reserving in our lives? Is there something we don't quite want to submit to Jesus? Is there some issue, some person, some thing, that we are afraid to waste on Jesus? The grace of this week is to submit all the objects of our love, every part of our hearts, to Jesus, and to say to him: Jesus, you are my only love!

PRAYER

O my God, I love you above all things with my whole heart and soul, because you are all good and worthy of all my love. I love my neighbor as myself for the love of you. I forgive all who have injured me, and ask pardon for all the injuries I have caused others. Amen. (*Traditional Act of Love*)

GOSPEL

Reclining at table with his disciples, Jesus was deeply troubled and testified, "Amen, amen, I say to you, one of you will betray me." The disciples looked at one another, at a loss as to whom he meant. One of his disciples, the one whom Jesus loved, was reclining at Jesus' side. So Simon Peter nodded to him to find out whom he meant. He leaned back against Jesus' chest and said to him, "Master, who is it?" Jesus answered, "It is the one to whom I hand the morsel after I have dipped it." So he dipped the morsel and took it and handed it to Judas, son of Simon the Iscariot. After Judas took the morsel, Satan entered him. So Jesus said to him, "What you are going to do, do quickly." Now none of those reclining at table realized why he said this to him. Some thought that since Judas kept the money bag, Jesus had told him, "Buy what we need for the feast," or to give something to the poor. So Judas took the morsel and left at once. And it was night.

When he had left, Jesus said, "Now is the Son of Man glorified, and God is glorified in him. If God is glorified in him, God will also glorify him in himself, and he will glorify him at once. My children, I will be with you only a little while longer. You will look for me, and as I told the Jews, 'Where I go you cannot come,' so now I say it to you."

Simon Peter said to him, "Master, where are you going?" Jesus answered him, "Where I am going, you cannot follow me now, though you will follow later." Peter said to him, "Master, why can I not follow you now? I will lay down my life for you." Jesus answered, "Will you lay down your life for me? Amen, amen, I say to you, the cock will not crow before you deny me three times."

JOHN 13: 21-33, 36-38

ST. THOMAS AQUINAS

When John says, "Peter said to him," he indicates Peter's confidence. Peter had understood what our Lord had just said as expressing some doubt about the perfection of Peter's love. Love is perfect when one exposes oneself to death for a friend: "Greater love has no man than this, that a man lay down his life for his friends" (John 15:13). And so because Peter was ready to die for Christ, he declared that he was perfect in love when he said, "I will lay down my life for you," that is, I am ready to die for you. He really meant this, and was not pretending. Still, we do not know the strength of our own love until it meets some obstacle to be overcome: "I am not aware of anything against myself, but I am not thereby acquitted" (1 Cor 4:4).

After Christ said "you cannot follow me now," Peter was confident of his own strength and said that he could follow Christ and die for him. Our Lord checked him by saying, "Will you lay down your life for me?" *It is like saying: Think what you are saying. I know you better than you know yourself; you do not know how strong your own love is. So do not assume that you can do everything. "So do not become proud, but stand in awe" (Rom 11:20). A similar thought is found in Matthew (26:41): "The spirit indeed is willing, but the flesh is weak."*

Our Lord allowed Peter to be tempted and to fall so that when he became head of the Church he would have an unpretentious opinion of himself and have compassion for his subjects when they sinned: "For we have not a high priest who is unable to sympathize with our weakness, but one who in every respect has been tempted as we are, yet without sinning" (Heb 4:15). In Peter, some temptations grew into sins. But Christ was tempted as we are, not because he committed sin, but because the temptations were penal in character. (Comm. John, ch. 13, 8.1843, 1845)

REFLECTION

Though Judas is Christ's betrayer, consider Peter's role. Peter loves Jesus, as St. Thomas Aquinas points out, and so he wants to lay down his life for Jesus against any enemy. Yet, it is Peter himself who will become another betrayer, even if he thought himself above such reprehensible deception. Our Lord's prophecy to Peter is chilling: "Will you lay down your life for me? The cock will not crow before you deny me three times." Peter would go further than Judas who never denied that he knew Jesus. But Peter would claim to not even recognize Jesus, much less even than to have had a relationship with Jesus. What Judas gave up for money, Peter gave up for nothing, but to save face.

In spite of the treachery of Peter's fall, St. Thomas sees the hand of God at work. This event allowed Peter to recognize his utter dependence on Jesus. We refer to Peter as the first pope, the man who was given the responsibility to shepherd Christ's flock. He did, in the end, lay down his life for Jesus, crucified, but upside down (according to an old tradition) because he felt unworthy to share the cross in the exact manner as his Lord.

Peter teaches us that every sin may be forgiven when we repent, even the most horrible of crimes. Divine mercy is everlasting and without limit. If we have found ourselves in the shadow of Peter on account of betrayal of love, let us also find ourselves in the shadow of the healing cross of Christ through the sacraments.

PRAYER

Father, your Son gave himself completely for our salvation. Open our hearts to accept the gift of divine love which sets us free from our petty attachments and preoccupation with ourselves so that we may take him into the world for others to meet. Amen.

GOSPEL

One of the Twelve, who was called Judas Iscariot, went to the chief priests and said, "What are you willing to give me if I hand him over to you?" They paid him thirty pieces of silver, and from that time on he looked for an opportunity to hand him over.

On the first day of the Feast of Unleavened Bread, the disciples approached Jesus and said, "Where do you want us to prepare for you to eat the Passover?" He said, "Go into the city to a certain man and tell him, 'The teacher says, "My appointed time draws near; in your house I shall celebrate the Passover with my disciples.""" The disciples then did as Jesus had ordered, and prepared the Passover.

When it was evening, he reclined at table with the Twelve. And while they were eating, he said, "Amen, I say to you, one of you will betray me." Deeply distressed at this, they began to say to him one after another, "Surely it is not I, Lord?" He said in reply, "He who has dipped his hand into the dish with me is the one who will betray me. The Son of Man indeed goes, as it is written of him, but woe to that man by whom the Son of Man is betrayed. It would be better for that man if he had never been born." Then Judas, his betrayer, said in reply, "Surely it is not I, Rabbi?" He answered, "You have said so."

MATTHEW 26: 14-25

ST. THOMAS AQUINAS

Avarice being an exaggerated love for possessing riches, it is excessive on two counts. First of all it goes too far in keeping. In this regard callousness to mercy is born of avarice, in that a person's heart is not so softened by mercy as to come to the aid of the wretch out if his own resources. Secondly, it is the part of avarice to go too far in getting. . . . In another way avarice can be viewed as to its effect, whereby in order to acquire wealth the man of greed employs now force—which entails violence, now deceit. Should the deceit be perpetrated verbally, where there is simple assertion, we have falsehood; where there is confirmation by oath, perjury. If the deceit is accomplished by deed, when it centers upon some object, it is fraud; on persons, treachery, as is clear from Judas' betrayal of Christ out of greed. (ST IIa–IIae, q. 118, a. 8 [G])

REFLECTION

The fact of Judas's betrayal is overwhelming. How could he have handed over his friend and Lord for a sum of money? How could Judas pretend to be with Jesus, all the while planning treachery in the darkness of his heart? How could he use a kiss, the mark of loving friendship, as a way to mark Christ for the soldiers in the garden of Gethsemane?

It is known that Judas used to steal from the money held in common by disciples of our Lord (John 12:6, 13:29). St. Thomas Aquinas helps us to understand that Judas's betrayal was the fruit of the vice of avarice, being too attached to having wealth. Considering that Christ and the apostles lived simply and poorly, they could not have had much money. So, one does not need to have a great deal to be avaricious. One may be willing to be a traitor for a very little. Political history proves the point many times over.

But let us not be taken too much with pointing our accusing fingers at Judas, and all the while miss the opportunity for repentance for our own callous refusals to be merciful to others by hoarding our time or relaxations or other pleasures and possessions, or for pushing to get more for ourselves in various, sometimes even small, deceitful ways. Let us stop looking at the guilt of the Judases we spot all around us while remaining blind to our own treacheries of one sort or another.

Rather, let us face ourselves in confession, and, like the "good thief" crucified beside Jesus, beg mercy. Let us trade the kiss of death Judas gave to Jesus for the kiss of Christ's feet as we approach the cross to adore it on Good Friday. Let us go to the core of the issue and hand over ourselves to Christ who handed himself over for our sake. Then we will be able to "hand over," that is, to share Christ, with all those God has placed in our lives.

PRAYER

Lord Jesus, Son of the Living God, I cry out: have mercy on me, a sinner. Amen.

PASCHAL
TRIDUUM

GOSPEL

Jesus came to Nazareth, where he had grown up, and went according to his custom into the synagogue on the sabbath day. He stood up to read and was handed a scroll of the prophet Isaiah. He unrolled the scroll and found the passage where it was written:

The Spirit of the Lord is upon me,
because he has anointed me
to bring glad tidings to the poor.
He has sent me to proclaim liberty to captives
and recovery of sight to the blind,
to let the oppressed go free,
and to proclaim a year acceptable to the Lord.

Rolling up the scroll, he handed it back to the attendant and sat down, and the eyes of all in the synagogue looked intently at him. He said to them, "Today this Scripture passage is fulfilled in your hearing."

LUKE 4: 16-21

† The Chrism Mass is the annual Mass when the bishop blesses the oils that will be used for the sacraments throughout the year in the diocese.

ST. THOMAS AQUINAS

God wished to produce his works in likeness to himself, as far as possible, in order that they might be perfect, and that he might be known through them. Hence, that he might be portrayed in his works, not only according to what he is in himself, but also according as he acts on others, he laid this natural law on all things, that last things should be reduced and perfected by middle things, and middle things by the first [things], as Dionysius says (Ecclesiastical Hierarchy, v). Wherefore that this beauty might not be lacking to the Church, [God] established [the sacrament of] Order in her so that some should deliver the sacraments to others, being thus made like to God in their own way, as co-operating with God; even as in the natural body, some members act on others. (ST Suppl., q. 34, a. 1 [Benz.])

REFLECTION

At the Chrism Mass the bishop, with the clergy of his diocese gathered with him, blesses the oils to be used for the sacraments: the oil of catechumens for those undergoing baptism, oil of the sick for the sacrament of anointing of the sick, and sacred chrism used at baptism, confirmation, and holy orders.

God has given us the sacraments and priests to administer them out of his mercy and desire to draw us into union with himself. As Christ was anointed through the power of the Holy Spirit, so are we at baptism. By the gift of the power of the Holy Spirit, Christ continues his sanctifying work through the priests who are anointed by the same Holy Spirit to make present the Body and Blood of Jesus in the Eucharist and to give us the other sacraments so necessary for our salvation.

It is at this Mass that the bishop invites the priests to renew their dedication to serve Christ and the Church. The Chrism Mass on Holy Thursday morning is a most fitting day for this renewal for it is the day when our Lord Jesus gave priestly power to the apostles in the Upper Room at the Last Supper and First Eucharist. While it is important to pray for priests every day, today we give special thanks to God for the gift of the priesthood without which we would not have the opportunity to be fed on Christ's Body and Blood, Soul and Divinity.

PRAYER

Lord Jesus Christ, you are the High Priest anointed by the Holy Spirit to bring blessings to us who are poor and in need of your divine grace; you free us from the bondage of sin and enlighten our minds to know you; you give us the grace of charity to love you above all things; you draw us to yourself that we may enjoy the peace and eternity of heaven. You do all these things through your appointed mediators, your holy priests. Bless them with your abundant gifts that they may continue faithfully in their work as your chosen ones; through them lead us to your throne where we may worship you in the fullness of life. Amen.

GOSPEL

Before the feast of Passover, Jesus knew that his hour had come to pass from this world to the Father. He loved his own in the world and he loved them to the end. The devil had already induced Judas, son of Simon the Iscariot, to hand him over. So, during supper, fully aware that the Father had put everything into his power and that he had come from God and was returning to God, he rose from supper and took off his outer garments. He took a towel and tied it around his waist. Then he poured water into a basin and began to wash the disciples' feet and dry them with the towel around his waist. He came to Simon Peter, who said to him, "Master, are you going to wash my feet?" Jesus answered and said to him, "What I am doing, you do not understand now, but you will understand later." Peter said to him, "You will never wash my feet." Jesus answered him, "Unless I wash you, you will have no inheritance with me." Simon Peter said to him, "Master, then not only my feet, but my hands and head as well." Jesus said to him, "Whoever has bathed has no need except to have his feet washed, for he is clean all over; so you are clean, but not all." For he knew who would betray him; for this reason, he said, "Not all of you are clean."

So when he had washed their feet and put his garments back on and reclined at table again, he said to them, "Do you realize what I have done for you? You call me 'teacher' and 'master,' and rightly so, for indeed I am. If I, therefore, the master and teacher, have washed your feet, you ought to wash one another's feet. I have given you a model to follow, so that as I have done for you, you should also do."

JOHN 13: 1-15

ST. THOMAS AQUINAS

Then when the Evangelist says, "Then he poured water into a basin . . . ," he describes Christ's service, and shows his admirable humility in three ways. First, as to what kind of service it was, for it was very lowly, since the Lord of majesty stooped down to wash the feet of his servants. Secondly, as to the number of things he did, for he put water into the basin, washed their feet, and then dried them. Thirdly, as to the way it was done: for Christ did not do it through others or with their help, but by himself. "The greater you are, the more you must humble yourself" (Sir 3:18).

As for the mystical meaning, three things can be gathered from these events. First, the pouring out of Christ's blood on the earth is indicated by his pouring water into the basin. For the blood of Jesus can be called water because it has the power to cleanse: "He washed us from our sins in his own blood" (Rev 1:4). And so blood and water came out of his side at the same time to show us that his blood washes away sins. Or, water can indicate the passion of Christ, for in Scripture water signifies tribulations: "Save me O God! For the waters," that is, tribulations, "have come up to my soul" [Ps 69:1]. Therefore, "he poured water into a basin," that is, he impressed the memory of his passion on the minds of the faithful by their faith and devotion: "Remember my affliction and my bitterness, the wormwood and the gall!" (Lam 3:19). (Comm. John, ch. 13, 2.1747, 1748)

REFLECTION

In giving us this gospel passage on the night of the institution of the Most Holy Eucharist, the Church desires that we reflect on the great love of Christ. His utter humility is proved both in the task reserved for lowly servants, the pouring of water for the washing of feet, and in the pouring of his Blood, begun sacramentally in this meal and culminating on Good Friday on the Cross.

St. Thomas draws our attention to these words and actions whose utter importance is underscored by the fact that they are Jesus' last.

There is no more important message of love than this final divine insistence of Christ that he makes us his friends, precisely through his incarnation, passion and death, resurrection and ascension. He washes us, cleanses us of our sins, and then feeds and nourishes us with his own Body and Blood that we might become what we eat and drink. He has done and continues to do all this for one very simple reason: to make us truly human again, and even divine. He humbly teaches us the meaning of being genuinely human, of rising above our animalistic tendencies, but also of refraining from overreaching as prideful Adam did when he reached for the forbidden fruit. Neither base desires nor prideful "lording it over others" is human. Christ is the perfect man, the perfect image of what it is to be human. And so, tonight we learn from his loving humility that we may truly give of ourselves for others, kneeling before them in service. We can do this, not in mere imitation of Christ, but by the transformation that comes from the most precious gift he has left us: himself in the Most Holy Eucharist. Here we meet him personally and are made one with him and his body, the Church. No mere human love, this! Only the Divine One makes it possible for us to pour out ourselves with him, first having made us know that we become Love through Holy Communion.

PRAYER

"O Sacred Banquet, in which Christ is received, the memory of his Passion is recalled, the soul is filled with grace, and the pledge of future glory is given to us. Help us, we beg you, so to reverence the sacred mysteries of your Body and Blood that we may constantly experience in our lives the fruit of your redemption." Amen. —*St. Thomas Aquinas*

GOSPEL

Jesus went out with his disciples across the Kidron valley to where there was a garden, into which he and his disciples entered. Judas his betrayer also knew the place, because Jesus had often met there with his disciples. So Judas got a band of soldiers and guards from the chief priests and the Pharisees and went there with lanterns, torches, and weapons. Jesus, knowing everything that was going to happen to him, went out and said to them, "Whom are you looking for?" They answered him, "Jesus the Nazorean." He said to them, "I AM." Judas his betrayer was also with them. When he said to them, "I AM," they turned away and fell to the ground. So he again asked them, "Whom are you looking for?" They said, "Jesus the Nazorean." Jesus answered, "I told you that I AM. So if you are looking for me, let these men go." This was to fulfill what he had said, "I have not lost any of those you gave me." Then Simon Peter, who had a sword, drew it, struck the high priest's slave, and cut off his right ear. The slave's name was Malchus. Jesus said to Peter, "Put your sword into its scabbard. Shall I not drink the cup that the Father gave me?"

So the band of soldiers, the tribune, and the Jewish guards seized Jesus, bound him, and brought him to Annas first. He was the father-in-law of Caiaphas, who was high priest that year. It was Caiaphas who had counseled the Jews that it was better that one man should die rather than the people.

Simon Peter and another disciple followed Jesus. Now the other disciple was known to the high priest, and he entered the courtyard of the high priest with Jesus. But Peter stood at the gate outside. So the other disciple, the acquaintance of the high priest, went out and spoke to the gatekeeper and brought Peter in. Then the maid who was the gatekeeper said to Peter, "You are not one of this man's disciples, are you?" He said, "I am not." Now the slaves and the guards were standing around a charcoal fire that they had made, because it was cold, and were warming themselves. Peter was also standing there keeping warm.

The high priest questioned Jesus about his disciples and about his doctrine. Jesus answered him, "I have spoken publicly to the world. I have always taught in a synagogue or in the temple area where all the Jews gather, and in secret I have said nothing. Why ask me? Ask those who heard me what I said to them. They know what I said." When he had said this, one of the temple guards standing there struck Jesus and said, "Is this the way you answer the high priest?" Jesus answered him, "If I have spoken wrongly, testify to the wrong; but if I have spoken rightly, why do you strike me?" Then Annas sent him bound to Caiaphas the high priest.

Now Simon Peter was standing there keeping warm. And they said to him, "You are not one of his disciples, are you?" He denied it and said, "I am not." One of the slaves of the high priest, a relative of the one whose ear Peter had cut off, said, "Didn't I see you in the garden with him?" Again Peter denied it. And immediately the cock crowed.

Then they brought Jesus from Caiaphas to the praetorium. It was morning. And they themselves did not enter the praetorium, in order not to be defiled so that they could eat the Passover. So Pilate came out to them and said, "What charge do you bring against this man?" They answered and said to him, "If he were not a criminal, we would not have handed him over to you." At this, Pilate said to them, "Take him yourselves, and judge him according to your law." The Jews answered him, "We do not have the right to execute anyone," in order that the word of Jesus might be fulfilled that he said indicating the kind of death he would die. So Pilate went back into the praetorium and summoned Jesus and said to him, "Are you the King of the Jews?" Jesus answered, "Do you say this on your own or have others told you about me?" Pilate answered, "I am not a Jew, am I? Your own nation and the chief priests handed you over to me. What have you done?" Jesus answered, "My kingdom does not belong to this world. If my kingdom did belong to this world, my attendants would be fighting to keep me from being handed over to the Jews. But as it is, my kingdom is not here." So Pilate said to him, "Then you are a king?" Jesus answered, "You say I am a king. For this I was born and for this I came into the world, to testify to the truth. Everyone who belongs to the truth listens to my voice." Pilate said to him, "What is truth?"

When he had said this, he again went out to the Jews and said to them, "I find no guilt in him. But you have a custom that I release one prisoner to you at Passover. Do you want me to release to you the King of the Jews?" They cried out again, "Not this one but Barabbas!" Now Barabbas was a revolutionary.

Then Pilate took Jesus and had him scourged. And the soldiers wove a crown out of thorns and placed it on his head, and clothed him in a purple cloak, and they came to him and said, "Hail, King of the Jews!" And they struck him repeatedly. Once more Pilate went out and said to them, "Look, I am bringing him out to you, so that you may know that I find no guilt in him." So Jesus came out, wearing the crown of thorns and the purple cloak. And he said to them, "Behold, the man!" When the chief priests and the guards saw him they cried out, "Crucify him, crucify him!" Pilate said to them, "Take him yourselves and crucify him. I find no guilt in him." The Jews answered, "We have a law, and according to that law he ought to die, because he made himself the Son of God." Now when Pilate heard this statement, he became even more afraid, and went back into the praetorium and said to Jesus, "Where are you from?" Jesus did not answer him. So Pilate said to him, "Do you not speak to me? Do you not know that I have power to release you and I have power to crucify you?" Jesus answered him, "You would have no power over me if it had not been given to you from above. For this reason the one who handed me over to you has the greater sin." Consequently, Pilate tried to release him; but the Jews cried out, "If you release him, you are not a Friend of Caesar. Everyone who makes himself a king opposes Caesar."

When Pilate heard these words he brought Jesus out and seated him on the judge's bench in the place called Stone Pavement, in Hebrew, Gabbatha. It was preparation day for Passover, and it was about noon.

And he said to the Jews, "Behold, your king!" They cried out, "Take him away, take him away! Crucify him!" Pilate said to them, "Shall I crucify your king?" The chief priests answered, "We have no king but Caesar." Then he handed him over to them to be crucified.

So they took Jesus, and, carrying the cross himself, he went out to what is called the Place of the Skull, in Hebrew, Golgotha. There they crucified him, and with him two others, one on either side, with Jesus in the middle. Pilate also had an inscription written and put on the cross. It read, "Jesus the Nazorean, the King of the Jews." Now many of the Jews read this inscription, because the place where Jesus was crucified was near the city; and it was written in Hebrew, Latin, and Greek. So the chief priests of the Jews said to Pilate, "Do not write 'The King of the Jews,' but that he said, 'I am the King of the Jews'." Pilate answered, "What I have written, I have written."

When the soldiers had crucified Jesus, they took his clothes and divided them into four shares, a share for each soldier. They also took his tunic, but the tunic was seamless, woven in one piece from the top down. So they said to one another, "Let's not tear it, but cast lots for it to see whose it will be," in order that the passage of Scripture might be fulfilled that says:

> They divided my garments among them,
> and for my vesture they cast lots.

This is what the soldiers did. Standing by the cross of Jesus were his mother and his mother's sister, Mary the wife of Clopas, and Mary of Magdala. When Jesus saw his mother and the disciple there whom he loved he said to his mother, "Woman, behold, your son." Then he said to the disciple, "Behold, your mother." And from that hour the disciple took her into his home.

After this, aware that everything was now finished, in order that the Scripture might be fulfilled, Jesus said, "I thirst." There was a vessel filled with common wine. So they put a sponge soaked in wine on a sprig of hyssop and put it up to his mouth. When Jesus had taken the wine, he said, "It is finished." And bowing his head, he handed over the spirit.

Here all kneel and pause for a short time.

Now since it was preparation day, in order that the bodies might not remain on the cross on the sabbath, for the sabbath day of that week was a solemn one, the Jews asked Pilate that their legs be broken and that they be taken down. So the soldiers came and broke the legs of the first and then of the other one who was crucified with Jesus. But when they came to Jesus and saw that he was already dead, they did not break his legs, but one soldier thrust his lance into his side, and immediately blood and water flowed out. An eyewitness has testified, and his testimony is true; he knows that he is speaking the truth, so that you also may come to believe. For this happened so that the Scripture passage might be fulfilled: *Not a bone of it will be broken.* And again another passage says: *They will look upon him whom they have pierced.*

After this, Joseph of Arimathea, secretly a disciple of Jesus for fear of the Jews, asked Pilate if he could remove the body of Jesus. And Pilate permitted it. So he came and took his body. Nicodemus, the one who had first come to him at night, also came bringing a mixture of myrrh and aloes weighing about one hundred pounds. They took the body of Jesus and bound it with burial cloths along with the spices, according to the Jewish burial custom. Now in the place where he had been crucified there was a garden, and in the garden a new tomb, in which no one had yet been buried. So they laid Jesus there because of the Jewish preparation day; for the tomb was close by.

JOHN 18: 1-40 & 19: 1-42

ST. THOMAS AQUINAS

Now, there are trees that have flowers and fruits all the time. In a similar way the tree of the Cross has flowers all the time. See that the wood of the Cross has produced a triple fruit. . . . First, the fruit of cleansing, because through the Cross we are liberated from sins. . . . Second, the fruit of sanctification, of which Romans 6:22 says: "You have fruit in sanctification." Of what does sanctification consist? It makes someone cling to the Cross. It is also true that man, alienated from God through sin, is reconciled through Christ. Thus we read in Rom. 5:10: "We are reconciled with God through the death of his Son." . . . So the ministers of the Church use the sign of the Cross in any sanctification. . . . Third, the fruit of glorification . . . Through sin humankind is excluded from paradise, and therefore Christ has suffered on the Cross, so that through the Cross the gate from the earthly things to the heavenly things would be open. Hence the Cross of Christ is signified by the ladder that Jacob saw. As we read in Gen. 28:12, Jacob saw the ladder, and its top touched the heavens, and he saw angels ascending and descending, and the Lord leaning on the ladder. All the saints go up to the heavens by the power of the Cross. (Sermon 18, *Germinet terra*, 3.-3.3, modified, in *Thomas Aquinas: The Academic Sermons*, vol. 11, The Fathers of the Church: Mediaeval Continuation, Washington, D.C.: The Catholic University of America Press, 2010)

REFLECTION

It was that very Cross that Judas fled. In the 2004 film, *The Passion of the Christ*, sometime after Judas betrays Jesus with a kiss he tries to undo that kiss by rubbing his lips raw on a stone pillar near where Jesus is being interrogated by Caiaphas. Another time Judas rubs his now-bloody lips on the moneybag containing the thirty pieces of silver before throwing it back to those who paid him to betray Jesus. If only Judas would have kissed the Cross of Jesus instead. Surely by kissing that wood he would be repenting of his sin rather than seeking some other wood from which he would hang himself.

Still visible at the Dominican Priory of San Marco in Florence, Italy is the exalted fresco by Fra Angelico of the crucifixion with St. Dominic kneeling at the foot of the Cross embracing it, or perhaps to use St. Thomas's words, *clinging to it*. Indeed, he appears to kiss the Cross. In this embrace and kiss, as St. Thomas teaches, is the power of sanctification.

To embrace the Cross is to make it the center of our lives. When we do this, we allow each moment of the day to be united to Christ and his Cross. We find in even the smallest annoyances, as well as the greater trials of life, opportunities to share in that Cross, to continue the embrace. It is for each one of us to discover the intimacy of embracing, even kissing, the Cross.

The power of sanctification that results is the exaltation of the person who clings to the Cross. It is, in a certain sense, the ongoing humanization and divinization of each one. Yet, such a transformation requires attachment to the Cross in a way similar to the electrical plug needing to be plugged directly into the outlet to draw the power of the electricity. Sanctification is the grace of becoming like God, which for each human being means becoming more like Christ, the perfect man and God. But to be most like Christ requires that we do as he did, to embrace the Cross, so as to know the power of the resurrection.

Mary is our greatest example of how to cling to the Cross and be holy. From the moment of the prophecy that the sword of sorrow would pierce her heart, until the last moment on which her Son hung on the Cross, she teaches how to stand and cling to the Cross because Jesus is there. Only Jesus can save us. In our worst moments, there is no safer or better place to be, because Jesus is there.

PRAYER

O thou Mother! fount of love!
Touch my spirit from above,
make my heart with thine accord:

Make me feel as thou hast felt;
make my soul to glow and melt
with the love of Christ my Lord.

Holy Mother! pierce me through,
in my heart each wound renew
of my Savior crucified:

Let me share with thee His pain,
who for all my sins was slain,
who for me in torments died.

Let me mingle tears with thee,
mourning Him who mourned for me,
all the days that I may live:

By the Cross with thee to stay,
there with thee to weep and pray,
is all I ask of thee to give.

—*Stabat Mater*, 13th century

GOSPEL

After the sabbath, as the first day of the week was dawning, Mary Magdalene and the other Mary came to see the tomb. And behold, there was a great earthquake; for an angel of the Lord descended from heaven, approached, rolled back the stone, and sat upon it. His appearance was like lightning and his clothing was white as snow. The guards were shaken with fear of him and became like dead men. Then the angel said to the women in reply, "Do not be afraid! I know that you are seeking Jesus the crucified. He is not here, for he has been raised just as he said. Come and see the place where he lay. Then go quickly and tell his disciples, 'He has been raised from the dead, and he is going before you to Galilee; there you will see him.' Behold, I have told you." Then they went away quickly from the tomb, fearful yet overjoyed, and ran to announce this to his disciples. And behold, Jesus met them on their way and greeted them. They approached, embraced his feet, and did him homage. Then Jesus said to them, "Do not be afraid. Go tell my brothers to go to Galilee, and there they will see me."

MATTHEW 28: 1-10

ST. THOMAS AQUINAS

Christ's resurrection was necessary . . . first of all, to fulfill the require-ments of divine justice by which those who humble themselves for God are exalted: "He has pulled down princes from their thrones and exalted the lowly" (Luke 1:52). Since Christ through charity and obedience to God humbled himself to the extent of death on the cross, it was necessary that he be exalted by a glorious resurrection. Consequently, the Psalmist speaks in the person of Christ and says, "You have known," that is you have approved of, "my sitting down," my "humility and passion, and my rising up," the glorification in my resurrection, as a gloss interprets this passage (Psalm 139:2). (ST IIIa, q. 53, a. 1 [G])

REFLECTION

St. Thomas knew it was essential to take nothing for granted with this great mystery of the resurrection. Others had been raised from the dead by Christ, although they eventually died again because they did not rise unto glory as Christ has. Thus, he dares to ask *whether* Jesus' resurrection was necessary. He even considers the argument that Christ accomplished our salvation through his passion and that there-fore nothing else was needed. While this might be true with certain distinctions, he says, Christ's resurrection was the first fruit and model of the good effects of his passion. One of those effects is the fulfilling of divine justice.

When we think of divine justice we usually associate it with pun-ishment for our sins. But divine justice works in the other direction as well, namely, God rewards virtue and most especially the virtues of humility and charity. St. Thomas gives this as the very first reason for the necessity of the resurrection, and this is worth a great deal of medi-tation. We tend to take the resurrection for granted. It's a given, almost a simple equation: Christ died, and Christ rose from the dead. It's too easy to be confined to thinking simplistically of Christ's resurrection as necessary just because he is divine. It's as if we tell ourselves: "Of course, Jesus would rise from the dead; after all, he's God and, well, no one can keep God down, so he had to resurrect." Such facile thinking prevents us from entering into the depth of the power of the resurrection.

To let God be God, to give God his due in our lives, is also a matter of justice. We owe it to him. From a human perspective, it might seem that that settles the issue. Except that, of ourselves, we're not able to give God his due. But for the superabundant generosity of God, we could never hope to rise above our state of being at enmity with God. Only in Christ's perfect and utterly obedient sacrifice is our debt to God fulfilled, not only for a moment, but for eternity. Furthermore, divine justice does not rest in the contentment of knowing a debt is fulfilled. One of the ways God proves his goodness is by doing what humans would consider superfluous: raising up, exalting, the lowly one who sought to fulfill his debt to God. This kind of divine love and justice (they cannot be separated) rewards Christ's dying in humble obedience with the most perfect exaltation: resurrection.

The end is the same for each person who lives in Christ through the sacraments, prayer and good works. Divine justice will have it no other way. Humble obedience before God necessitates being raised up, even as Christ was raised from the dead.

PRAYER

O God, in your swift justice you reach down to raise up the lowly and humble. Grant me the grace of serving you in perfect obedience by entering more deeply into the humble heart of Christ Jesus, your Son, especially through his sacrifice renewed on the altar at holy Mass. May I come to know the power of his resurrection in every moment of my life. Amen.

GOSPEL

When the sabbath was over, Mary Magdalene, Mary, the mother of James, and Salome bought spices so that they might go and anoint him. Very early when the sun had risen, on the first day of the week, they came to the tomb. They were saying to one another, "Who will roll back the stone for us from the entrance to the tomb?" When they looked up, they saw that the stone had been rolled back; it was very large. On entering the tomb they saw a young man sitting on the right side, clothed in a white robe, and they were utterly amazed. He said to them, "Do not be amazed! You seek Jesus of Nazareth, the crucified. He has been raised; he is not here. Behold the place where they laid him. "But go and tell his disciples and Peter, 'He is going before you to Galilee; there you will see him, as he told you.'"

MARK 16: 1-7

ST. THOMAS AQUINAS

Christ's resurrection was made known to men according to the way in which divine things are revealed. But this divine revelation depends upon diverse interior dispositions. Men who are well disposed understand these divine things in a truthful way; others ill disposed perceive these same things only with a mixture of doubt and error: "An unspiritual person is one who does not accept anything of the spirit of God" (1 Cor 2:14). This is why Christ appeared in his proper form to those who were well disposed to believe in him after his resurrection. (ST IIIa, q. 55, a. 4 [G])

REFLECTION

The account of the resurrection is not a fable that ends with some moral point to the story by which we are taught to be good. Quite the opposite: it is the most demonstrative act of God proving his lordship over this world and even death. Not that he needed to prove anything for himself. It has always been ourselves who have demanded the proof. It was to give testimony on the witness stand of our self-appointed and small-minded court of human affairs that he became a man, suffered and died for us.

Many, at the time of Christ, wanted their own proof, a proof of power that would have been weaker than the resurrection, really. Let him come down from that cross and then we will believe in him (Mark 15:31–32). For God, coming down from the cross would not have been the real overcoming of death.

The fact is that everyone left the courtroom before the testimony was finished. Christ's resurrection from the dead is his final proof that he is the Son of God and that we are good, not on account of our puny, pious, and often fraudulent, attempts to placate God, but because he loves us unto death. He truly and completely loves us even when we crucify him. He did all these things because we needed them in order to become fully human again.

Let us return to the courtroom of truth and have displayed for us the gospel accounts of the resurrection of Jesus Christ. Let us gain true knowledge of these events, entering deeper and deeper into the facts and the meaning of these facts. Let us not fear that the divine judge will call us as witnesses and that we will implicate ourselves in our own admission of guilt. Rather, let us freely acknowledge before this most humble and persistent of lovers that he is Life and Love. By this very surrender, we shall gain the necessary interior dispositions of which St. Thomas speaks. As this disposition of belief and trust in Christ deepens, we shall find ourselves saying with St. Paul: "I wish to know Christ and the power of his resurrection; likewise to know how to share in his sufferings by being formed into the pattern of his death. Thus do I hope that I may arrive at resurrection from the dead" (Phil 3:10–11).

We gain this truthful evidence when we ponder the Sacred Scriptures and when we contemplate their meaning in the light of the teaching of the successors of the Apostles, our holy bishops. Daily prayer is not an option if we are to arrive at the knowledge and experience of the power of the resurrection. And isn't that exactly what each of us longs for: the experiential knowledge, by the gift of the Holy Spirit of Wisdom, of entering personally into the power of Christ's resurrection? It's the key to being truly and fully human.

PRAYER

Lord Jesus Christ, I want to experience the power of your resurrection in the same way that the women at your tomb on the very first Easter did, and as your apostles did. Deepen in me the ability to enter more profoundly into the knowledge of you and all that you have done for us, so that I may be transformed by the very same power of your resurrection. Grant that I may ponder your holy word and receive you worthily in Holy Communion; that I may experience the effects of your redemption, and thus be allowed to behold the truth of your testimony and the beauty of your face in my mind throughout each and every day. Amen.

GOSPEL

At daybreak on the first day of the week the women who had come from Galilee with Jesus took the spices they had prepared and went to the tomb. They found the stone rolled away from the tomb; but when they entered, they did not find the body of the Lord Jesus. While they were puzzling over this, behold, two men in dazzling garments appeared to them. They were terrified and bowed their faces to the ground. They said to them, "Why do you seek the living one among the dead? He is not here, but he has been raised. Remember what he said to you while he was still in Galilee, that the Son of Man must be handed over to sinners and be crucified, and rise on the third day." And they remembered his words. Then they returned from the tomb and announced all these things to the eleven and to all others. The women were Mary Magdalene, Joanna, and Mary the mother of James; the others who accompanied them also told this to the apostles, but their story seemed like nonsense and they did not believe them. But Peter got up and ran to the tomb, bent down, and saw the burial cloths alone; then he went home amazed at what had happened.

LUKE 24: 1-12

ST. THOMAS AQUINAS

[Mary Magdalene] had the office of an apostle; indeed, she was an apostle to the apostles insofar as it was her task to announce our Lord's resurrection to the disciples. Thus, just as it was a woman who was the first to announce the words of death, so it was a woman who would be the first to announce the words of life. (Comm. John, ch. 20, 3.2519)

REFLECTION

Eve was, of course, the woman who had announced the words of death when she handed over the forbidden fruit to Adam (Gen 3:6). St. Thomas thinks it quite appropriate, therefore, that the female sex should be the first to learn about the resurrection and so bring news of it to Christ's chosen band of men. One cannot help but think of yet another woman whose "yes" to the angel Gabriel was both the antidote to Eve's disobedience and the beginning of that Life whose resurrection is now announced.

As a member of the Order whose primary work it is to preach the gospel, it could not have been lost on St. Thomas that Mary Magdalene was the first *preacher* of the resurrection when she brought this glorious word to those men who had fled their Lord and had hidden themselves away, cowering in fear. While preaching is the special charism of the Dominicans and the task of the bishops, priests, and deacons at Mass, all baptized and confirmed Christians are evangelizers, that is, bringers of the gospel to the world, especially to those who are cowering in shame and fear.

I suspect that when many Catholics hear this call to proclaim the Good News, they feel incapable, unprepared, daunted by the task. But it is no task, really. It is simply to do what each one of us does quite naturally, namely, to share with another our experience of happiness. For example, when we return from a vacation, we want to share the sights and sounds with our friends at home. The romantic lover cannot stop referring to the beloved. Even the child or young person cannot be inhibited when it comes to telling about his or her newest friend or discovery of something fun to do. In this sense, evangelization is the most natural thing in the world: telling others about the greatness and wonder of Jesus Christ. And, while it is a very human act, we can be sure that divine grace is ever present to assist us in doing what Mary Magdalene did when speaking to Jesus' disciples.

All this presupposes, of course, that we each have a real experience of Jesus in our lives. This real experience should not be based merely on subjective feelings alone. For we experience Christ objectively through the sacraments and the infusion of sanctifying grace. The Catholic in the state of grace *does* have a real experience of God. It is the work of daily prayer with and in the Church that brings all of the moments of one's life into contact with sanctifying grace.

The person who has come to know and love Jesus as the Christ, as Lord and Savior, finds it impossible *not* to bring him to others. Even if we do not speak explicitly at every moment about him, the conversion of our hearts to love, the experience of the power of his passion, death and resurrection, the knowledge of being united to him in divine friendship, are always implicitly coloring our every action and word. There is a qualitative difference in the life of the Christian. He or she is drawn more and more to converse with Almighty God, meets Christ more intimately through the sacraments—especially the Most Holy Eucharist—and listens with greater understanding to the Holy Spirit in the words of Sacred Scripture.

May we find in St. Mary Magdalene, patroness of preachers, and our Blessed Mother, the example of saying "yes" to Jesus interiorly and exteriorly, that we may bring Jesus and news of him to all our friends.

PRAYER

Lord Jesus Christ, draw me to yourself and most especially into your heart, that I may experience more and more your divine love and power. Take away all my fears, and heal all that prevents me from living fully in union with you and the Father and the Holy Spirit. Enliven me with your Holy Spirit, for this will be enough to make me your apostle. Use me in any way that you desire for the good of my family and friends. Amen.

EASTER
SUNDAY

GOSPEL

On the first day of the week, Mary of Magdala came to the tomb early in the morning, while it was still dark, and saw the stone removed from the tomb. So she ran and went to Simon Peter and to the other disciple whom Jesus loved, and told them, "They have taken the Lord from the tomb, and we don't know where they put him." So Peter and the other disciple went out and came to the tomb. They both ran, but the other disciple ran faster than Peter and arrived at the tomb first; he bent down and saw the burial cloths there, but did not go in. When Simon Peter arrived after him, he went into the tomb and saw the burial cloths there, and the cloth that had covered his head, not with the burial cloths but rolled up in a separate place. Then the other disciple also went in, the one who had arrived at the tomb first, and he saw and believed. For they did not yet understand the Scripture that he had to rise from the dead.

JOHN 20: 1-9

Alternative readings from Easter Vigil or LUKE 24:13-35 at an afternoon or evening Mass.

ST. THOMAS AQUINAS

According to Chrysostom's understanding, [Peter] saw the linen cloths so folded and arranged which would not have been the case if the body had been furtively snatched away; "and believed," with a true faith, that Christ had risen from the dead. What follows, "for as yet they did not know the scripture," refers to the statement, "he saw and believed." It was like saying: before he saw these things he did not understand the scripture "that he must be raised from the dead"; but when he saw he believed that he had risen from the dead. (Comm. John, ch. 20, 1.2489)

REFLECTION

Some people treat belief, particularly religious belief, as if to believe without personal scientific experience is contrary to human intelligence. Of course, believing the word of another as well as scientific evidence are two different but compatible modes of arriving at truth. Even scientists believe in the principle that truth exists, though "truth" cannot be put under a microscope. Moreover, they take on faith the principles of their respective sciences because they have not the time to prove for themselves all the experiments that have brought their scientific fields to a high level.

The resurrection of Christ is both a matter of faith and experience. We take the word of the witnesses as true, and Christ himself comes to us through the Sacred Scriptures and the sacraments of the Church and the teaching of the Magisterium.

The accounts of the apostles and the many others to whom Christ appeared after his resurrection from the dead are worthy of our belief. The Fathers of the Church have countered the many arguments against faith in these witnesses, but there is one that stands out as especially noteworthy. It is the fact that the apostles, except for St. John, all ran away and hid when Christ was condemned and crucified; how impossible it was for them to give of themselves to try to save him. They would not die for Jesus when he was most in need of them, yet each one gave witness with his very life that this dead man had risen from the dead.

Could these same men have died for a mere theory of resurrection, or for a fable, or for a lie? Not only these, but also the numerous others who died as martyrs those early years, not to mention the countless men and women through the ages who have come to know Jesus and have died for him.

It is not enough, however, that we give some simple assent to the likelihood that these witnesses did indeed see Jesus. It is, after all, not merely a page from history that explains the Incarnation, Passion, and Resurrection of Christ. He is the Son of God, and, as such, is owed the full affirmation that our being allows for so great a gift: the offer of being divinized. This kind of assent, though itself a grace from God, calls down yet more profound gifts, namely, the revelation that one makes to his friend. In this case, it is God who brings us more deeply into the interior of his divine existence, showing us with greater assurance what could never be proven even if we ourselves had stood at the empty tomb on that first Easter Sunday. It is this that the apostles experienced, as well as those hundreds of others during the days leading up to Christ's final appearance at the Ascension. Let us, then, say yes again and again so that we may be brought more and more into the heart of Christ. This is the faith of the Church. This is how we are saved. This is the assurance of our own resurrection unto the eternal wedding banquet in paradise.

PRAYER

Lord Jesus Christ, Son of the living God, I praise and thank you with all my heart for the power of your cross and resurrection. Draw me most close to your Sacred Heart in the midst of your Body, the Church. Let nothing inhibit my knowledge of you, my love for you. Enkindle more powerfully in my own heart the fire of the Holy Spirit that I may live, now and always, in your Father's house with the Blessed Virgin Mary and all the Saints. Amen.

Saint Thomas Aquinas, pray for us!

APPENDIX A:
CALENDAR OF LENT 2014–2023
& LECTIONARY CYCLE

Ash Wednesday–Easter

Year	Sunday Year	Lent	Date
2014	A	Ash Wednesday	March 5
		1st Sunday of Lent	March 9
		2nd Sunday of Lent	March 16
		3rd Sunday of Lent	March 23
		4th Sunday of Lent	March 30
		5th Sunday of Lent	April 6
		Palm Sunday	April 13
		Easter Triduum	April 17
		Easter Sunday	April 20
2015	B	Ash Wednesday	February 18
		1st Sunday of Lent	February 22
		2nd Sunday of Lent	March 1
		3rd Sunday of Lent	March 8
		4th Sunday of Lent	March 15
		5th Sunday of Lent	March 22
		Palm Sunday	March 29
		Easter Triduum	April 2
		Easter Sunday	April 5

Year	Sunday Year	Lent	Date
2016	C	Ash Wednesday	February 10
		1st Sunday of Lent	February 14
		2nd Sunday of Lent	February 21
		3rd Sunday of Lent	February 28
		4th Sunday of Lent	March 6
		5th Sunday of Lent	March 13
		Palm Sunday	March 20
		Easter Triduum	March 24
		Easter Sunday	March 27
2017	A	Ash Wednesday	March 1
		1st Sunday of Lent	March 5
		2nd Sunday of Lent	March 12
		3rd Sunday of Lent	March 19
		4th Sunday of Lent	March 26
		5th Sunday of Lent	April 2
		Palm Sunday	April 9
		Easter Triduum	April 13
		Easter Sunday	April 16

Year	Sunday Year	Lent	Date
2018	B	Ash Wednesday	February 14
		1st Sunday of Lent	February 18
		2nd Sunday of Lent	February 25
		3rd Sunday of Lent	March 4
		4th Sunday of Lent	March 11
		5th Sunday of Lent	March 18
		Palm Sunday	March 25
		Easter Triduum	March 29
		Easter Sunday	April 1
2019	C	Ash Wednesday	March 6
		1st Sunday of Lent	March 10
		2nd Sunday of Lent	March 17
		3rd Sunday of Lent	March 24
		4th Sunday of Lent	March 31
		5th Sunday of Lent	April 7
		Palm Sunday	April 14
		Easter Triduum	April 18
		Easter Sunday	April 21

Year	Sunday Year	Lent	Date
2020	A	Ash Wednesday	February 26
		1st Sunday of Lent	March 1
		2nd Sunday of Lent	March 8
		3rd Sunday of Lent	March 15
		4th Sunday of Lent	March 22
		5th Sunday of Lent	March 29
		Palm Sunday	April 5
		Easter Triduum	April 9
		Easter Sunday	April 12
2021	B	Ash Wednesday	February 17
		1st Sunday of Lent	February 21
		2nd Sunday of Lent	February 28
		3rd Sunday of Lent	March 7
		4th Sunday of Lent	March 14
		5th Sunday of Lent	March 21
		Palm Sunday	March 28
		Easter Triduum	April 1
		Easter Sunday	April 4

Year	Sunday Year	Lent	Date
2022	C	Ash Wednesday	March 2
		1st Sunday of Lent	March 6
		2nd Sunday of Lent	March 13
		3rd Sunday of Lent	March 20
		4th Sunday of Lent	March 27
		5th Sunday of Lent	April 3
		Palm Sunday	April 10
		Easter Triduum	April 14
		Easter Sunday	April 17
2023	A	Ash Wednesday	February 22
		1st Sunday of Lent	February 26
		2nd Sunday of Lent	March 5
		3rd Sunday of Lent	March 12
		4th Sunday of Lent	March 19
		5th Sunday of Lent	March 26
		Palm Sunday	April 2
		Easter Triduum	April 6
		Easter Sunday	April 9

APPENDIX B:
SELECTIONS FROM THE
WRITINGS OF SAINT THOMAS AQUINAS

Ash Wednesday	*ST* IIa–IIae, q. 111, a. 2 [G]
Thursday	*Comm. John,* ch. 12, 4.1643
Friday	*ST* IIa–IIae, q. 147, a. 1. and a. 3 [G]
Saturday	*ST* IIIa, q. 65, a. 1 [G]
1st Sunday A	*ST* IIIa, q. 41, a. 1 [G]
1st Sunday B	*ST* IIIa, q. 41, a. 2, ad 2 [G]
1st Sunday C	*ST* Ia, q. 114, a. 5 [G]
Monday 1	*Catechetical Instructions: The Apostles' Creed, a. 7*
Tuesday 1	*Catechetical Instructions: The Lord's Prayer*
Wednesday 1	*ST* Suppl. q. 1, a. 1 [Benz.]
Thursday 1	*ST* IIa–IIae, q. 83, a. 15, ad 2 [G]
Friday 1	*ST* IIIa, q. 49, a. 3, ad 2[G]
Saturday 1	*ST* IIa–IIae, q. 25, a. 8 [G]
2nd Sunday A	*ST* IIIa, q. 45, a. 1 [G]
2nd Sunday B	*ST* IIIa, q. 45, a. 4 [G]
2nd Sunday C	*ST* IIIa, q. 45, a. 3, ad 3 [G]
Monday 2	*ST* IIIa, q. 84, a. 10, sed contra [G]
Tuesday 2	*ST* IIa–IIae, q. 162, a. 1, corpus, ad 2 [G]
Wednesday 2	*ST* IIa–IIae q. 161, a. 2, ad 2 [G]
Thursday 2	*ST* IIa–IIae, q. 117, a. 2 [G]
Friday 2	*ST* Ia, q. 2, a. 3, ad 1 [G]
Saturday 2	*ST* IIIa, q. 49, a. 5, corpus, ad 4 [G]
3rd Sunday A	*Comm. John,* ch. 4, 2.577
3rd Sunday B	*Comm. John,* ch. 2, 2.392
3rd Sunday C	*ST* Ia, q. 21, a. 3, ad 2 [G modified]
Monday 3	*ST* IIIa, q. 42, a. 2, ad 1 [G]
Tuesday 3	*ST* IIIa, q. 84, a. 10, corpus [G])
Wednesday 3	*Catechetical Instructions: The Lord's Prayer*
Thursday 3	*ST* IIa–IIae, q. 104, a. 3 [G modified]
Friday 3	*ST* IIa–IIae, q. 44, a. 5 [G]

Saturday 3	*ST* IIa–IIae, q. 82, a. 3 [G]
4th Sunday A	*Comm. John,* ch. 9, 1.1311
4th Sunday B	*Comm. John,* ch. 3, 2.475, 3.480
4th Sunday C	*ST* IIa–IIae, q. 30, a. 2 [G]
Monday 4	*Comm. John,* ch. 4, 7.690
Tuesday 4	*Comm. John,* ch. 5, 1.716
Wednesday 4	*Comm. John,* ch. 5, 5.796
Thursday 4	*Comm. John,* ch. 5, 6.824
Friday 4	*Comm. John,* ch. 7, 3.1067
Saturday 4	*Comm. John,* ch. 7, 5.1115
5th Sunday A	*Comm. John,* ch. 11, 4.1519–20
5th Sunday B	*Comm. John,* ch. 12, 4.1645
Monday 5 Years A and B	*Comm. John,* ch. 8, 1.1133
Monday Year C	*Comm. John,* ch. 8, 2.1144–45
Tuesday 5	*Comm. John,* ch. 8, 3.1191
Wednesday 5	*Comm. John,* ch. 8, 4.1199
Thursday 5	*Comm. John,* ch. 8, 8.1287
Friday 5	*Comm. John,* ch. 10, 6.1453, 1468
Saturday 5	*Comm. John,* ch. 11, 7.1569
Passion Sunday A	*Comm. John,* ch. 12, 3.1620–21
Passion Sunday B	*Comm. John,* ch. 12, 3.1622
Passion Sunday C	*Comm. John,* ch. 12, 3.1627
Monday of Holy Week	*Comm. John,* ch. 12, 1.1599
Tuesday of Holy Week	*Comm. John,* ch. 13, 8.1843, 1845
Wednesday of Holy Week	*ST* IIa–IIae, q. 118, a. 8 [G]
Chrism Mass	*ST* Suppl., q. 34, a. 1 [Benz.]
Holy Thursday	*Comm. John,* ch. 13, 2.1747, 1748
Good Friday	Sermon 18, *Germinet terra,* 3.-3.3
Holy Saturday-Vigil Mass A	*ST* IIIa, q. 53, a. 1 [G]
Holy Saturday-Vigil Mass B	*ST* IIIa, q. 55, a. 4 [G]
Holy Saturday-Vigil Mass C	*Comm. John,* ch. 20, 3.2519

SUGGESTIONS FOR FURTHER READING

SAINT DOMINIC

Bedouelle, Guy, O.P. *Saint Dominic: The Grace of the Word*. San Francisco: Ignatius Press, 1987.

Dorcy, Sr. Mary Jean, O.P. *Saint Dominic*. Rockford, Ill.: Tan Publishers, 2009.

Jarrett, Bede, O.P. *The Life of St. Dominic*. New York: Doubleday, 1995.

Koudelka, Vladimir, O.P., ed. *Dominic*. Translated by Consuelo Fissler and Simon Tugwell, O.P. London: Darton, Longman and Todd, 1997.

Vicaire, M.-H., O.P. *Saint Dominic and His Times*. Green Bay, Wisc.: Alt Publishing Company.

DOMINICAN SAINTS

Bedouelle, Guy, O.P. *In the Image of Saint Dominic: Nine Portraits of Dominican Life*. San Francisco: Ignatius Press, 1994.

Dorcy, Sr. Mary Jean, O.P. *St. Dominic's Family*. Rockford, Ill.: Tan Publishers, 2009.

Novices of the Dominican House of Studies. *Dominican Saints*. Rockford, Ill.: Tan Publishers, 2009.

HISTORY OF THE ORDER OF PREACHERS

Coffey, Reginald M., O.P. *The American Dominicans: A History of*

St. Joseph's Province. Washington, D.C.: Mt. Vernon Publishing Company, 1970.

Hinnebusch, William A., O.P. *The History of the Domincan Order.* 2 vols. Staten Island: Alba House, 1966.

Mulchahey, M. Michele. *"First the Bow is Bent in Study": Dominican Education before 1350.* Toronto: Pontifical Institute of Mediaeval Studies, 1998.

DOMINICAN SAINTS AND SPIRITUALITY

Hinnebusch, William A., O.P. *Dominican Spirituality: Principles and Practice.* Washington, D.C.: The Thomist Press, 1965.

McDermott, Thomas, O.P. *Catherine of Siena: Spiritual Development in Her Life and Teaching.* New York: Paulist Press, 2008.

Murray, Paul, O.P. *The New Wine of Dominican Spirituality: A Drink Called Happiness.* London: Burns and Oates, 2006.

Raymond of Capua. *The Life of Catherine of Siena.* Translated by Conleth Kearns, O.P. Washington, D.C.: Dominicana Publications, 1980.

Torrell, Jean-Pierre, O.P. *Christ and Spirituality in St. Thomas Aquinas.* Translated by Bernhard Blankenhorn, O.P., and Robert Royal. Washington, D.C.: The Catholic University of America Press, 2011.

Tugwell, Simon, O.P., ed. *Early Dominicans: Selected Writings.* New York: Paulist Press, 1982.

Undset, Sigrid. *Catherine of Siena.* San Francisco: Ignatius Press, 1954.

SAINT THOMAS AQUINAS

Chesterton, G. K. *St. Thomas Aquinas: The Dumb Ox.*

Torrell, Jean-Pierre, O.P. *Saint Thomas Aquinas: Volume 1, The Person and His Work.* Translated by Robert Royal. Washington, D.C.: The Catholic University of America Press, 1996.

———. *Volume 2, Spiritual Master.* Translated by Robert Royal. Washington, D.C.: The Catholic University of America Press, 2003.

INTERNET
RESOURCES

The Order of Preachers Web site available at
http://www.op.org/en

The Dominicans of the Saint Joseph Province
(Eastern Province) Web site available at
http://www.ordopraedicatorum.org

The Blog and Journal of the Dominican Student Brothers
Web site available at
http://www.dominicanablog.com

ABOUT THE
AUTHOR

Dominican Father Paul Jerome Keller was ordained to the priesthood on May 21, 1993 in Washington D.C. for the Province of St. Joseph. He acquired a Bachelor and Licentiate in Sacred Theology at the Pontifical Faulty of the Immaculate Conception in Washington D.C., and a Doctorate specializing in sacramental theology at Sant' Anselmo in Rome.

Fr. Keller is presently the Assistant Professor of Sacramental Theology at Mt. St. Mary's of the West Seminary in Cincinnati and has previously taught at Providence College in RI and Franciscan University of Steubenville in Ohio. He presents numerous lectures, conferences and seminars on a large array of subjects, including the sacrament of Reconciliation, the Holy Mass, Liturgical Worship, spiritual conferences, and the Rosary throughout the United States. Father Keller has made guest appearances on Relevant Radio, the Catholic Channel on Sirius Radio, Vatican Radio, and Catholic Answers Live, discussing various subjects. He also has experience in pastoral work, having served for a number of years as parochial vicar at St. Mary's Church in New Haven, Connecticut.

Fr. Keller is the past president of The Society for Catholic Liturgy, a multidisciplinary association of Catholic scholars, teachers, pastors, and professionals. He is also the author of *101 Questions & Answers on the Sacraments of Healing: Penance and Anointing.*